ABBOTSBURY revisited

A fresh look at

"An Appreciation of Abbotsbury"

published for the Ilchester Estate Trustees

in 1973 by Messrs William Bertram & Fell,

Architects and Surveyors, Bath

Nigel Melville

Abbotsbury, 2006

FOREWORD

I am delighted to have been asked to write a foreword, on behalf of Mrs Townshend, to the "Abbotsbury Appreciation Revisited" prepared by Nigel Melville. Looking back at the Foreword written by Lady Teresa Agnew (Mrs Townshend's mother) to the original Appreciation document in 1973, it is clear that the Family have always taken a great interest in the village and its future.

The original Appreciation endeavoured to offer a strategy of how the best interests of the Estate and the people of Abbotsbury could be protected and enhanced It is clear, by studying the village today, that the strategy that was subsequently implemented by the Family was a huge success.

Nigel's updated Appreciation deals only with the village property. A number of issues dealt with in the original Appreciation relating to architectural design, enhancement, development and building conversions continue to present the Estate with challenges and, I imagine will continue to do so for the foreseeable future.

The "Appreciation Revisited" is an interesting modern record setting out the position in the village today and in due course it too will become an historical record which will also be an important reference document.

I would like to take the opportunity, on behalf of the Estate, to thank Nigel for his efforts and hard work.

Marcus K Scrace
General Manager
Ilchester Estates

INTRODUCTION

Taking a fresh look at the "Appreciation of Abbotsbury"

Thirty years ago, according to one who lived here at the time, moving to Abbotsbury was like returning to the dark ages, and there are passages in the Parish Council minutes of those days which bear that out. In 1972, the Rural District Council asked the Ilchester Estate, owners of the village, to connect 24 cottages to the main sewer at the rate of 8 per month. Though the sewer had been provided in 1968, there were still 80 properties (out of 130 in the village) waiting to be connected.

But change was already afoot ~ on 17th September, 1971, Mr Edwards of the Estate spoke to the Parish Council about *"the problems of dealing with repairs; the cost of improving the whole village would be £250,000"*. And the whole village ~ or as near as made no difference ~ belonged to the Estate: at the time of the District Council's Village Plan in 1974, the Estate owned 110 of the 130 buildings in the village. 18 of them were occupied by estate workers or their widows, 28 were held on lease, 40 were on monthly tenancies, 12 were let along with farms, and 12 were empty. A survey of the 120 employed residents carried out five years earlier showed that, in rank order ~

> 35 people worked in service industries
> 29 worked in farming or fishing
> 17 were Estate workers
> 14 worked in local or national government
> 12 worked in manufacturing
> 8 worked in transport, and
> 5 were builders or contractors.
> (No record is given of the number of children or unemployed people but 24% of the village population were retired at the time.)

The real changes had in fact already begun in the early 1970's, when the Estate drew up *"a battle plan to save the village"* which envisaged a furniture workshop, a glassware works, and a veterinary surgery. That was not enough to stop the District Council claiming in the Village Plan that *"there is a great deal wrong with many of the buildings. Most of the cottages are small, and many lack the basic sanitary and other amenities considered necessary by the owners and now required by the Public Health Authority."*

The Estate's battle plan, however, involved more than putting in a few small-scale industrial or commercial units. Much more.

The Trustees of the Estate instructed their Land Agents to carry out a thorough survey of the village: Messrs William Bertram and Fell were appointed to prepare what they called *"An Appreciation of Abbotsbury"*. Peter Fell, ARICS, surveyed every single building in the village, from the humblest shed up to the Tithe Barn, while Benedict Blathwayte photographed every one of them. The end product is a remarkable document, a record of the start of Abbotsbury's journey in to modern times.

Miraculously, the negatives from the Appreciation have survived, along with Peter Fell's original handwritten notes. Thanks to the support of Edward Green of the Ilchester Estate, I was able to spend a day going through the background material, and borrow the negatives. When the Abbotsbury Heritage Research Project was set up in 2004, I decided that revisiting the buildings survey would be my contribution to the Project's web site (*www.abbotsbury-heritage.org.uk*). Simon Thompson of Dorset Community Action then suggested that my researches should be published for a wider audience.

What I have tried to do here is not to imitate the Appreciation survey (far less the historical introduction which is still the best source of its kind for information on Abbotsbury's past), but simply to take a look, thirty years down the line, at what has happened to the buildings of the village.

Nigel Melville

References and acknowledgements

Apart from the obvious one ~ the people who live here today ~ there are four main sources of information on Abbotsbury's buildings. Rather than repeat their titles in full I have given them shorthand names :

"The Inventory" ~ HMSO: the Royal Commission on the Historic Monuments of England (West Dorset), published in 1952.

"The Appreciation" ~ the Bertram and Fell survey of 1973-74.

"The Conservation Plan" ~ quotations from Heaton, MJ and Keevil, GD, 2003, "Abbotsbury Abbey, Dorset: A Conservation Plan" (non-publication planning report, Ilchester Estates and English Heritage)

"Dave Stevens" ~ postcards from the unique collection gathered by Dave Stevens, Chairman of the Abbotsbury Heritage Research Project, some of which have been published in *"Greetings from Abbotsbury"* (ed. Paul Atterbury, Postcard Press, 2004)

I am grateful to Benedict Blathwayte for permission to reproduce his 1973 photographs, to Peter Fell for so carefully preserving the negatives for over thirty years, and to Marcus Scrace for patiently reading through the text in draft, suggesting many positive changes, and writing the foreword.

NOTE

I have used as titles the names given to each property in the Appreciation, and only added contemporary names where it helps to identify properties.

I have also followed the route that the original writers followed, even when that might seem illogical on the page now.

NM

Swan Inn

New Vicarage (Swan Lodge)

(Scheduled in the 1974 Village Plan as a building which the Secretary of State had agreed to include in the statutory list)

Not the first pub to bear the name ~ the original Swan Inn was further down Rodden Row, about where the Abbotsbury Studio now stands.

Graham Roper took over as landlord in 1966: at the time there were two petrol pumps at the pub, brought there from the garage in West Street along with Bill Hughes, who was the Swan landlord during the war years. Graham retained the pumps for 15 years or so, earning some criticism from the Appreciation for his efforts ~ *"as you move into the village the first things you see are a clutter of signs and petrol pumps outside the Swan Inn. The new car park ... is bald and one feels that some planting would improve the scene"*. Graham and Sue have done a lot to improve that scene, and the car park mentioned in the Appreciation is now a garden area.

Graham Roper rebuilt the skittle alley (where village pantomimes were once staged every year) in 1977, using local volunteers as his work force, and the pub never closed during the alterations. Similarly, in 1991, the bar was redecorated by volunteers between 3.00pm and 7.00pm on a Sunday afternoon.

Today the Swan hosts the community computers, and has acted as the base for several courses in basic IT skills, as well as being the home of the Tourism and Traders Association and the Beachcombers fund-raisers.

In 2005, the Swan skittle alley housed a crowded village meeting to protest against plans to close the road to Weymouth for major works during April and May (the work was eventually done at night and finished ahead of schedule).

Graham Roper, landlord of the Swan Inn, bought the vicarage in 1978, and turned it into a guesthouse. It was built in 1962, and was described as a "new building" in the Appreciation. The solar panels in the roof are even newer, and only the cross inset in the front gable reveals its church origin. The current vicarage, like the vicar, is now in Portesham.

Incidentally, why "Rodden Row" ? The obvious answer might be that this is the road leading to Rodden village, but that is more true today than it would have been years ago, and in any case it doesn't lead directly to Rodden. One theory put forward in the course of researching for this book is that "rodden" is a Celtic word for "red soil" ~ that sounds feasible, but while the soil around here is sometimes red, it's not particularly so here in Rodden Row. Alternatively, one of the studies prepared for the Estate in 2002 noted that *"another name found for Rodden Row is Sheep Street, perhaps because sheep were regularly driven along it, or penned there for sale"*. That, however, still doesn't entirely explain the name.

3 and 5 Rodden Row

*(Scheduled in the 1974 Village Plan as a building which
the Secretary of State had agreed to include in the statutory list)*

5 Rodden Row may at one time have housed a tannery: according to Dave Stevens, there were once some outbuildings at the back which have since been demolished, and there was certainly a small slaughterhouse in Back Street.

The village had a saddler and at least one boot maker (William Cornick, listed in the 1871 and 1875 trade directories), so there would have been a market for tannery products.

7 to 11 Rodden Row

*(Scheduled in the 1974 Village Plan as a building which
the Secretary of State had agreed to include in the statutory list)*

The Appreciation describes this as a *"massive nineteenth century building ... in sharp contrast to the terraces opposite"*, which sounds negative, but the author adds *"the contrast between the two groups of buildings adds to the interest of the scene"*.

The terrace was built by the Earl of Ilchester to replace earlier, thatched, cottages, a smithy and the original Swan Inn after a disastrous fire at the end of the 19th century, and has generally housed workers on the Ilchester Estate, though the stationmaster of the Abbotsbury branch line lived here at one time.

Reading Room & WI Hall (Abbotsbury Studio)

1973

2005

(Scheduled in the 1974 Village Plan as a building which the Secretary of State had agreed to include in the statutory list)

The predecessor of the Reading Room was the original Swan Inn, seen in the picture below, from Dave Stevens' collection ~ it appears in the trade directories for 1871 and 1875 and on the OS map of 1889, but was burnt down shortly afterwards, with the rest of the terrace. It was replaced in 1890 by the Reading Room (men only!) and the terrace on the previous page. James Knight appears in the 1881 census as a blacksmith and licensed victualler and again in the 1891 census as an innkeeper, but Phoebe Cosins, listed as an infant school mistress in 1881 had by 1891 become "charge of club in reading room".

The building was still a WI hall in 1982, when the Estate hoped that the WI would move to the Strangways Hall, so that the reading room could be *"let for a workshop enterprise"*: then it became a workshop for Mr Hickmott, an upholsterer.

John Skinner opened it as his studio in 1991, and lived through an outcry in 1994, when he placed a nude male figure in the garden: overnight, it was clothed in a nappy, and eventually made to face away from the road, but not before it attracted the attention of Auberon Waugh in the *Daily Telegraph*. A similar figure attracted comment nearly 10 years later, but sensitivities were not so readily moved on that occasion. John moved to the south of France in 2005, and a new artist has taken over the Studio.

Not clearly visible in either photo is the square bracket mounted on a stout pole in the studio garden ~ the last vestige of the street lights that once graced the village before they were dismantled in 1943 and the glass put to use in a local greenhouse.

(loaned by Dave Stevens)

13 Rodden Row

1973

2005

The author of the Appreciation clearly didn't like this house, describing it as a *"1940's villa, completely out of character"* (but it is at least twenty years older than that), and asking the quite reasonable question *"How did a bow fronted villa come to be built in one of the most attractive streets in Abbotsbury ?"*

The present occupants have done all they can to improve the appearance of the house ~ white soffits and window frames with black guttering and down pipes have taken the place of the all-green paintwork on doors, windows, gutters and pipe work that was here in 1973, and the mass of pebble-dash has been broken down by the use of slates on the two bay windows.

15 Rodden Row

(Grade II listed in 1956 as a pair with no. 17)

For many years this was the Estate Manager's house ~ the 1871 and 1875 trade directories and the 1881 census all record Mark Hopson ("Land Agent"), his wife, four children and a general servant living here, but in 1891 and 1901, the "Clerk of Works (Estate)" was James Hutchings, presumably a bachelor in 1891 as only his name is entered for the house. By the time of the 1901 directory, however, he was married happily enough to have five children.

Mark Hopson had been replaced by James Hutchings by 1889, who was still in post fifty years later, as his name appears in the directory for 1939. By the 1950's, the clerk of works was still a Tim Hutchings, occupying the office on the left of the door, while Peter Limm used the one on the right.

The house became the Awen Gallery when Courtney Davis used it as his studio and gallery for Celtic art before moving to Salway Ash. It then became, until 2004, a gallery for Chapel Yard Pottery before reverting to being a private house.

17 Rodden Row

(Grade II listed in 1956)

The mid-19th century house appears in the 1939 trade directory as *"refreshment rooms"*, run by Mrs Harry Pittman. Their son Ted lived here all his life, working as a woodman and gravedigger on the Estate. (Long before 1939, Elizabeth Critchell was listed as a *"boarding house keeper"* in the 1901 census and as running *"refreshment rooms"* in the 1903 directory ~ but as Abbotsbury houses were not numbered at that date, she could just as probably have lived next door in no. 19.)

No. 17 may seem to have been built at the same time as no. 15 on its left, but the dressed stones at the join of the two houses suggests that this was an infilled property. There is a theory that at one time there may have been an entrance to the Abbey precinct here, or perhaps to the cottages, mentioned below, which once stood between here and the parish church.

When the present occupant started renovation work, he discovered the flue for his neighbour's Aga behind his fireplace, he uncovered the tops of walls in odd positions and he found a void between this house and no. 19. The fact that Rodden Row changes direction slightly at this point might not be obvious from the road, but it makes for an oddly-shaped bathroom at the rear of the house.

Behind the house once stood an array of tiny cottages, all of which disappeared in the 19th century fire which put an end to the Rodden Row smithy and the original Swan Inn.

19 Rodden Row

21 Rodden Row

(Listed Grade II in 1956)

(Grade II listed in 1956)

This was at one time the village school, and became "Mrs Gill's Tea Rooms" (run, despite the name, by Mrs Beale) in the 1920's through to 1939, according to the trade directories for those years. The Beales were the last couple to run a tearoom from this house. In the 1950's and later, members of several Abbotsbury families, still represented in the village lived and worked here, next door, and two doors away in the Estate Office at no. 15.

When no. 19 was a school, it was a "Penny School", so called because the children had to pay a penny a week to attend.

The west wall of the house still contains an original mullion window, probably dating from its construction in the 17th century (though its listing puts it as 18th century), but now covered in and left in situ when the house was linked to the much more recent houses next door. The inglenook fireplace exposed in a 1989 restoration contains many dressed stones thought to be from the Abbey. The western gable wall shows what seems to be a double gable ~ the dressed corner stones on the corner of the house lie inside a second wall, which forms the link with no. 21. A curious arrangement, with no obvious explanation, other than the possibility that the linking wall relates to earlier houses now replaced by the 19th century terrace leading to the corner of Rodden Row and Church Street.

Listed as part of the block including 1-5 Church Street. According to the Appreciation, this is a *"typical 1830's house"*, but it is perhaps more likely that it is one of the *"great many neat slate roofed cottages"* (p. 23 of the Appreciation) that were built at around the same time as the Earl of Ilchester put up the new school, i.e. in 1858. The listing record puts the house as *"mid-19th century"*.

26 Rodden Row (Abbotsbury Tea Rooms)

1973

2005

(Grade II listed in 1956)

At the time of the 1889 OS map, this was the village Post Office and general stores, and an Edwardian postcard in Dave Stevens' collection shows the Market Street frontage exactly as it remains to this day.

William and Jane Gibbons appear in the trade directories for 1889 and 1903 as *"postmaster/ironmonger"*, but by 1939 William Wickwar is listed as *"stationer/Post Office"*. House numbering didn't arrive in Abbotsbury until the 50's, so that directory puts this building down as 2 Market Street, while it was listed Grade II as "Threeways, 26 Rodden Row".

The 1950's photograph below, from the same collection may throw some light on the confusion ~ the two side-by-side doors clearly imply that there were once two houses here, one facing on to Market Street, and the other one in Rodden Row.

The Inventory describes the building as *"built late 17th century with subsequent repairs"*, and the Appreciation notes that it was at that time (1973) being rebuilt. By then a new window had been inserted and that second door had been walled up. Run as an antique shop, it became a tearoom in 1996 and changed hands in 2004.

(loaned by Dave Stevens)

The building has never been far from controversy, thanks to its position on a junction that grows harder to negotiate as vehicles grow larger. As early as April 1926, the Parish Council drew the County Council's attention to *"the necessity of placing suitable notices in the village as a warning more especially to motorists and cyclists to drive slowly and cautiously upon approaching the dangerous corner at the lower end of Rodden Row, Market Street and Church Street, and opposite the Public Schools."* By November of the same year, a "danger notice" had been fixed in Rodden Row, but the 30 mph speed limit didn't arrive until 1938.

In 1970, the Parish Council even debated the extraordinary proposal that *"the County Surveyor be asked if he could purchase the house and shop at the junction of Rodden Row and Market Street, and pull it down to make the corner wider. The property was up for sale and in a bad state of repair."* The Appreciation tackled the issue head-on in 1973 and concluded that *"if one adopts the premise that Abbotsbury is very pleasant as it is, and should be altered as little as possible then there does not seem to be any magic solution to the traffic problem. It seems likely that as long as there is traffic, Abbotsbury will have a traffic problem."*

That problem arose dramatically in 2004 when a coach driver misjudged the corner and impaled his vehicle on scaffolding erected by thatchers, closing the road for several hours while the scaffolding firm dismantled their work and freed the coach and its cargo of pensioners. At least now, in 2005, part of the problem has been tackled by a pair of signs in Rodden Row, warning drivers of long vehicles that turning left is tricky, and that oncoming vehicles may be encountered in the middle of the road.

Below, another view of those two doors ~ 50 years or so earlier than the one opposite.

(loaned by Dave Stevens)

20 to 24 Rodden Row

(Grade II listed in 1956 and now listed as "20 and 22 Rodden Row")

The 1889 OS map shows a solid line of houses from the corner up to the entrance to Dansel's yard: the space on the left was once a cottage that has since disappeared, with only the vestiges of its much lower roofline as evidence that it has ever been there. It had gone by the date of the Inventory when these cottages were described as *"three tenements ... built probably early in the 18th century."* The pair are the only three-storey thatched houses in the village, but as the Appreciation comments it *"does not look out of scale because it is built on lower ground and the roof line follows that of the two storey terrace.'* The old builders knew their territory.

No's. 22 and 24 (on the left, with the porch) were converted into one cottage by a Mr & Mrs Finch. During the work, a 1729 farthing was found in the house, and the lath walls were found to be covered in layers of newspapers, cloth and wallpaper. Papers dating from 1872 were also found during the building work, and on the kitchen wall were measurements for a coffin. The blocked-up window above the porch has been re-opened, and the ground floor window has been extended to take the place of the left-hand door. The Appreciation says that this was *"apparently once the Post Office"*, but is confusing it with no. 26 on the corner, or the fact that a telephone kiosk once stood next door.

No. 20 (on the right), once the home of James Mundy, a naval pensioner, was restored by Mr & Mrs Wood ~ as the first couple to take up a lease on a property for restoration, they were offered a peacock for Christmas lunch by the Estate: it duly arrived, trussed for the oven, with the feathers separately packed. The restoration made the columns of the Dorset Echo at the time. According to the Appreciation, the windows and arches are later than the original structure, though one local resident thinks the window glass is the oldest in the village. The house has changed hands several times, most recently in 2000.

In each case, the houses were in very poor condition before the new occupants took on the restoration.

Estate Yard (Dansel)

(Scheduled in the 1974 Village Plan as a building which the Secretary of State had agreed to include in the statutory list ~ it was later scheduled for listing as "Barns in Strangways Estate Yard")

"Dansel" stands for Danielle and Selwyn Holmes, whose gallery celebrated its 25th anniversary in August 2004, when they told the story of the gallery in the *Chesil Magazine* ~

"In 1979, Edward Green, who was Estate Manager in charge of lettings at the time, was advised that the many buildings in need of restoration should not all be turned into residential accommodation, but some should be converted for business use to encourage local employment and to help keep the school open, showing that the village was alive and moving forward. The only other craftsman in the village at that time was Roger Gilding, the potter, on West Street. Other than that there was the Post Office Stores, the antique shop on the corner, the butcher, the Swan Inn and the Ilchester Arms.

We were looking to move our existing workshop from Eype near Bridport as it was too small, and we were put in touch with the Estate by CoSIRA (the Council for Small Industries in Rural Areas) and were given the opportunity to take on what used to be the Old Estate Yard, to use as a woodworking workshop and showroom. It was converted by the Estate who put big glass windows behind the existing old stable doors and knocked through walls in order to make one long space.

/continued overleaf

(continued from p. 13)

At first we just made furniture to commission, but soon realised that the many visitors to Abbotsbury wanted to buy smaller cheaper things so we soon put the offcuts to good use. We could not feasibly make enough different designs on our own, so we started selling other people's work. After discussions with the potter and then Greg Shepherd, who had started his glass engraving workshop at the Wheelwrights, we all decided we would only sell work in our own medium so as not to step on each other's toes. This has turned out to be a very good discipline as Dansel Gallery has now become one of a very few 'only wood' shops in the country. Now more than 200 woodworkers are represented, probably the largest concentration of its kind in the country. The gallery houses a superb collection of high quality hand-made items from British designer-craftsmen with the emphasis on good design and high quality of finish. 40% of the craftsmen are from the South West, many of them from Dorset.

In 1990 the workshop was moved from Rodden Row to 10a West Street to allow more space for larger pieces of furniture to be displayed and to produce more work to sell to other shops around the country, until finally in 1998 the workshop left the village to go back to Eype where it all started, and where Selwyn still produces pieces for the gallery."

18 and 16 Rodden Row

1973

2005

(Both these cottages were listed Grade II in 1956)

The whole of Rodden Row is described in the Inventory as "a range of seven tenements ... built at different times late in the 17th century" and are described as "18th century" in the listing register. The 1881 census showed 160 people living in Rodden Row, not including two houses that were marked as uninhabited: the population had dropped to 122 in 1891 and to 92 in 1901. Today's equivalent is probably less than 40.

Until 1953, when the house changed hands, the tenant of no. 18 was a Miss Critchell, perhaps related to the Elizabeth Critchell who is described in the 1881 census as a widow of 70, working as a garden labourer, or the Critchells who ran a boarding house across the road. In 1953, no. 18 was a two-bedroom cottage with a single living room downstairs on one side of the entrance lobby and a coal store on the other. There was no bathroom, only a "bungalow bath" hung up by the back door, and a privy at the back of the house. Everything happened in the living room ~ the bath was filled up for use there from a Burco boiler in the tiny kitchen, and all the family meals were set there, even though it was so draughty that one could see the curtains moving in the wind. It was only modernised in the 1970s, when the coal store was made into a decent room, the kitchen became a bathroom and a new kitchen was added: it was apparently one of the last Estate workers' cottages to be modernised.

In that same year of 1953, the new tenant for no. 18 lived in no. 16, along with his parents, sister and grandfather in what is still a two-bedroom cottage. The family originally came from Bruton in Somerset, but had a brother in the village, living in West Street. Of the same age and original design as no.18, the house was modernised rather later in the 1970's, when the ground floor was made into one large room and a kitchen and bathroom were added at the rear. It has since housed a variety of tenants, including several Estate shepherds.

14 Rodden Row (Wheelwrights)

1973

2005

(Listed Grade II in 1956)

(loaned by Daphne Sheppard)

The building is known today as "Wheelwrights" in recognition of its history. When the author of the Appreciation was baffled by the appearance of a "garage door" at such a high level, he was nearer the truth than he guessed: the door did, in fact, lead to a garage. Though described as "18th century", what appears to be "1616" is carved on one of the chimney stacks.

Samuel Mundy (standing by the door in the c.1900 photo on the left) and Joseph Stoodley both appear in the 1881 census for Rodden Row, and in the trade directories of 1871 and 1875 as coopers: in the 1889 and 1903 directories, Samuel Mundy appears as "wheelwrights/reading room", and by 1939 John Mundy is listed as a wheelwright. John Mundy worked here as a wheelwright, cooper, blacksmith and undertaker until around 1942: the wheelwright side of the business might have had to end in 1935, when the Parish Council asked to have the ramp (which had been used to bring carts into the building) removed, as it *"extended a full 6 feet into the roadway."* The ramp, however, stayed in place for several more years.

One of the apprentices here in the 1880s was Harry Vine Norman, who was funded by Lord Ilchester to train as a missionary in China, where he was martyred in front of his burned-out church during the Boxer Rising. Several of his family, as well as members of the wheelwright's family, still live in Dorset and have visited Wheelwrights with stories of the old days. During the war, the Mundy family housed evacuees from the Bassett area of Southampton.

The Inventory claims that *"the building has had the openings renewed and the front plastered".* It does appear to have a rendered front in some old photos, and the Appreciation notes that it had been recently repointed with cement mortar.

In a tape made in 2001, Greg Shepherd described how they took over the workshop in 1981 in a state of dereliction, with earth floors and green algae on the walls. Over the next five years, they virtually rebuilt both the cottage and the adjoining workshop. The timber vice formed from a tree growing out of the workshop wall may have gone, and the plaited-straw-and-plaster ceilings have been replaced with plasterboard, but the medieval cob and timber wall is still there behind the plaster board as you enter today's tearoom. *"We spent the last of our youth working on that cottage"* remembers Greg.

Their business was described by Anthony Howard in *"Country Ways Companion"* in 1988, where he writes that the Shepherds' order book included 10 Downing Street and Buckingham Palace. Greg Shepherd speaks of selling their work to Margaret Thatcher and several members of the Royal Family, as well as to Harrods and Garrards the jewellers.

The shop window fronting the street depicts Sam Mundy from the photograph opposite, and the little cart that Greg etched is called "Josie Rose" to celebrate the birth of their first child in 1986.

In 1988, the Shepherds emigrated to Australia ~ returning to Abbotsbury after a winter holiday in Spain, *"it was the strangest thing, as if we had never set foot there: the Estate is so old that all of us just pass through it. Perhaps we had done our time; if we had left a mark on the cottage, it would only be a very small part, for all the generations that had lived there."* But they describe their time in Abbotsbury as a privilege ~ *"we were watching the end of an era; the modernisation had not yet started"* ~ and even 20 years later, the Shepherds remember the kindness of the villagers and add that their heart and soul still stay in the village. Their taped message ended *"You're in a home loved by two people who never ever dreamt of leaving."*

It was to be 17 years before they returned to Abbotsbury, spending two days here in the summer of 2005 to meet old friends and show their elder daughter the house where she had been born. Looking round the cottage, Greg said of their decision to leave in 1988 ~ *"when we came back from Spain, we just felt that the house didn't recognise us."*

When the Shepherds left, the stock was taken over by a signwriter, who later moved up the road to no. 10, which eventually became the Bear Shop. Wheelwrights then became a baker's shop and café, and in 1996 Sue and Nigel Melville turned it into a tearoom and tea garden (selected as "a hidden treasure" by American magazine *British Heritage*), and a showplace for textile art.

12, 10 and 8 Rodden Row

(Grade II listed in 1956 as no's 10 and 12)

6 Rodden Row

(Grade II listed in 1956 as no's 6 and 8)

All three of these cottages, along with no. 6, are described in the listings register as "18th century with much refenestration", which is the technical way of saying that the windows have been altered since the cottages were built. It's a word that crops up quite a lot in the register.

No. 12, on the left, has always been a private house, occupied by Mr Limm who worked for the Estate and as a chimney sweep (the last resident sweep in the village), then by Roger Pitman, a professional musician in the UK and overseas, from 1990 to 1995. It must be one of the smallest cottages in the village, consisting of a single room on each floor with lean-to extensions at the back to provide a kitchen, shower room and toilet. The garden is perhaps three times the size of the cottage. The house has been rethatched since 1973 and no longer has the dipped section over the door.

No. 10, in the centre, has been a sign-writer's studio, where customers could also buy the glassware from the business at Wheelwrights and then, from 1994 to 2004, it was the home of "Abbotsbury Bears and Friends", opened by the then owners of the Old School House Tea Room in the square. It is currently (2006) available for let as a retail unit. It has also been re-thatched, presumably at the same time as no. 12 ~ the ridge of the new thatch is considerably lower than the original, because the earlier thatch had been built up layer upon layer over the years until it had become simply too thick and too heavy for the roof timbers. The new, straighter, line of thatch has meant that this cottage no longer has the "eyebrows" over the first floor windows.

No. 8, on the right, (only just included in the Appreciation picture, above left) has since been incorporated into a single house with no. 6 (see the next picture), and greatly modernised since the late 1990's.

This is another of the houses in Abbotsbury that has been created by joining two former cottages into one, which may go some way to explain the very much higher population in the village a century ago. In this case, it was already joined up to no. 8 (the half-glassed door on the left) when the present occupants moved here in the late 1990's, but it was considerably modernised by them. Although of an age with the rest of Rodden Row, it is not clear why thatch has given way to slate for these end three cottages, though it has been said that a roof blaze prompted the change.

2 and 4 Rodden Row

(Grade II listed in 1956, as "cottage in row, formerly two")

The photographs are more than a little confusing ~ the porched doorway in each of them belongs to what is now called 2 Rodden Row, but was originally the right-hand one of two porches, each serving a tiny cottage: the one-time left-hand porch is now a small window. There was also, many years ago, a door to a third cottage, which is just visible by the corner in the left-hand photograph, but has long since weathered in and is today largely concealed by the shrubs. The right-hand end of the terrace is now part of no. 1 Rosemary Lane.

No. 2 was turned into a single house in the 1970's, before the Appreciation. Even so, there was still restoration work to be done in the late 1980's when it changed hands once more: the house was full of Marley tiles, which all had to be ripped out and removed.

At that time (c. 1988/89) all the gardens on this side of Rodden Row were open at the back, and the area behind them may at some time have been the village dump ~ certainly there was a great deal of scrap iron there, as well as blue and white china.

1 Rodden Row (1 Rosemary Lane)

(Scheduled in the 1974 Village Plan as a building which the Secretary of State had agreed to include in the statutory list as "2 Rosemary Lane and adjoining barns", having formerly been included in the supplementary list)

This was never 1 Rodden Row (that's the Swan Inn) ~ compare the early 20th century photograph, below left, with the contemporary view, above right, and notice how the little Regency-style porch has moved around over the years, finding a new home when the house (which was always 1 Rosemary Lane) was incorporated into the end cottage in Rodden Row.

The building on the right, now part of the house, was one of the village's bakeries, run by Charles Toms (below right) from at least 1903 to 1939: it is still possible to see where the old ovens stood. A lean-to shed by where the old garage stood, farther up the lane, was where the horse and cart for the rounds were kept.

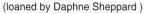

(loaned by Daphne Sheppard)   (loaned by Rosemary Rees)

East Farm: Small barn on Rodden Row

1973  **2005**

Virtually lost to view now by the Russian vine, not called the "mile-a-minute" vine for nothing, but nonetheless a colourful softening agent for the barn.

Buildings on north side of farmyard

1973  **2005**

In the earlier photograph, there is only one central door, but the change of use to stables has greatly improved both the look and the usefulness of the block.

Barn at corner of Rodden Row/Rosemary Lane

1973  **2005**

(Scheduled in the 1974 Village Plan as a building which the Secretary of State had agreed to include in the statutory list as "Barns at East Farm on corner of Rosemary Lane and Rodden Row [one on corner only]")

Remarkably unchanged in 30 years, though the creeper is staking its claim on the roof here too. The roof is currently (2006) being renewed.

Barn attached to south end of house

1973  **2005**

(See East Farm house for details of the barn's listing)

Here, too, the greenery ~ this time it's Virginia creeper ~ was in full leaf when the right-hand photograph was taken. It has been here for a century or more, and has the curious habit of spreading in alternate directions over a 20-year cycle. More than once, the Appreciation makes the point that hedges and wall-coverings such as this add to the charm of the village scene.

Farm house (No. 2 Rosemary Lane) (East Farm)

(Grade III listed according to the Appreciation and scheduled for listing in the Draft for the village plan, with the note that it was "formerly included in the supplementary list")

East Farm is a traditional Dorset longhouse (where a single building originally sufficed for family and livestock), but evidence in the loft space suggests that it has never been thatched, despite its age and traditional layout. The family here have bred competition horses.

The Appreciation's description of East Farm house adds *"5 hideous concrete garages in yard with aluminium up and over doors"* ~ hideous they may be, and they are still here, but the blame doesn't lie with East Farm.

~ ~ ~ ~ ~

Next door to East Farm, but long gone, was the cottage (below, left and right) of "Granny Clack", more formally Mabel Claxton who, even as a very elderly lady (she died in her 90's a little over a decade ago), was known for her sprightly performance of a "broom dance". Fortunately for her health, she had moved out of the cottage before the roof unexpectedly fell in.

(loaned by Dave Stevens)　　　(loaned by Dave Stevens)

Garage opposite East Farm (Rowan Cottage)

The shed with the corrugated iron roof to the left of the garage in the earlier photograph was where Mr Toms, the baker at 1 Rosemary Lane, used to keep his horse and cart.

The garage, which had previously been part of East Farm, was replaced in 1990 by what is now called Rowan Cottage, amid some controversy over the height of the roofline, the builder apparently demanding compensation if he were forced into removing and lowering the roof.

3 and 5 Rosemary Lane

1973 / 2005

(Grade III listed according to the Appreciation and scheduled for listing in the 1974 village plan, with the note that it was "formerly included in the supplementary list")

Sid Price, stationmaster at Abbotsbury, lived in 5 Rosemary Lane when this house was two separate cottages. (Frank Toms lived in no. 3) According to one of Mr Price's relations, the family kept chickens under the stairs, and relied on a well in the garden. Despite restoration work when the houses were combined, the original oak lintel to the open fireplace, which once caught fire, remains. The house was still considered to be two cottages at the time of the Appreciation, and because of its status, the present owners have not been permitted to remove the door to one of them. The cobbles in front of the cottage were mentioned in the Appreciation and have survived to this day, but the "old elm stumps" mentioned then are no longer so visible.

The picture below shows how little - and yet how much - things have changed in the 80 years or so since it was taken. At the time of that picture, the open doors of the cottages appealed to passing sheep and cows, one cow on its way to milking once managing to get itself stuck in the doorway.

(loaned by Daphne Sheppard)

1a Hands Lane

1973 / 2005

This was at one time the police house for the village: the Rural District Council bought it in 1971, along with the surrounding land, with a view to erecting some bungalows for elderly people.

The walls of the house were white at the time of the Appreciation, which recommended that they be toned down, as the house was very visible from the western approach to the village ~ though it is not clear from monochrome photographs, it seems that the advice was heeded, as the house is now a more muted cream colour.

1-10 Hands Lane

1973

2005

15 Back Street

1973

2005

(Grade III listed in 1973, and now listed Grade II)

This row of houses was first proposed by Dorchester Rural District Council in 1944. The Parish Council criticised the idea, because the site stood higher than the water reservoir outlet, opened on to a muddy road, and were on Glebe land. Perhaps they were right: the Appreciation comments that the group *"has none of the sensitivity in form or the affinity with its natural surroundings which the local craftsmen gave their own vernacular architecture"*. However, they went up in the early 1950's, and were originally intended only for agricultural workers.

In 1956, the tenant of a house in West Street complained to the Parish Council that somebody had jumped the queue for one of the Hands Lane houses ~ it emerged that the rival claimant had been allocated the house by Council officers without consultation either with the Housing Committee or the Parish Council, and the system was then tidied up. Following changes in the law, however, some of the houses have been bought and come on the market from time to time at prices probably beyond the reach of the intended original occupants.

Unlike the traditional Abbotsbury house, these all have front gardens, and they are built well above the shelter of the valley. It is interesting, though, that traditional styles and materials have returned in the construction of the garden walls, and the maturing trees have done much to soften the original atmosphere of the little estate.

Described as "derelict" in the Appreciation, but with a note that *"since survey the house has been 'done up'"* ~ according to the Inventory, the 18th century house has "modern brick segmented heads" to the windows. The garden wall in the right-hand photograph was rebuilt in 2004.

Thirty years after the Appreciation, the Estate's care for its Abbotsbury cottages was highlighted in the *Daily Telegraph* as one of the reasons why buyers should look at this house: as to "why not", the paper bluntly warned *"full of tourists in the summer ..."* and concluded with an awful pun ~ *"would suit weekender who likes swanning about in the country."*

In the 1920's, this cottage belonged to a Mr Dunford (a relation of the thatcher who worked from the "Basket Factory" further down Back Street) who acted as coal merchant to the village, storing the coal that he had delivered by rail from Weymouth in his outhouses, and selling it round the village from a horse and cart.

(For a much earlier view of 15 Back Street, see the photograph overleaf.)

Barn west of 15 Back Street

1973

2005

This barn and the one in the next picture are both now part of the post-Appreciation house called The Keep, described later in the book (p. 87).

Barn west of last photo

1973

2005

This barn and the one in the previous picture are both part of the post-Appreciation house called The Keep, described on p. 87.

This one was once Albert Stokes' butcher's shop, but as the photographs below show, it later became a stable and was originally twice its present size: in the shop days, the butcher used to smoke hams in the big open fireplace. The map in the Inventory shows what looks like a continuous line of properties between 13 and 15 Back Street, implying that there had as recently as the 1940's been more substantial development here ~ and the right-hand photograph below (taken well before the 40's) confirms that impression.

(loaned by Iris Trevett)   (loaned by Dave Stevens)

13 and 11 Back Street (Spring Cottage)

(Grade II listed in 1956)

This was originally two cottages ~ the door for no.13 can be seen in the left-hand photograph. One villager can remember looking at them with a view to purchase, before they were rebuilt as one house in 1975; and "rebuilt" is apparently the best word, as the building had to be nearly razed to the ground and built afresh. The listings register describes the building as 18th century with 20th century reconstruction and renewed fenestration, a reference to the fact that the Estate were keen to keep the traditional cottage style, and to resist the temptation of the time to put in bigger windows. The house changed hands in 2005.

Basket Factory

(Grade II listed in the Appreciation and described as "an attractive little building")

According to Dave Stevens' book, the little building is known as the Spar House, because it was the workshop of Mr Dunford the thatcher: spars are the lengths of split hazel used to hold the thatch in position. According to Judy Nash (*"Thatchers and Thatching"*, Batsford 1991), a spar-maker could make up to 2000 spars on a wet day, while one man once made 250 in 40 minutes for a competition. Basket-making, though, was a spare-time occupation for thatchers, and a 1920s card in the Dave Stevens collection shows Mr Dunford at work on a large basket in front of his "factory". According to the Appreciation, back in 1973 *"next door in no. 11 lives a man in his seventies whose father was a thatcher and used the little workshop for basket making."*

Was this where Moses Cousins lived ? It could be: it is described in the listing as 18th century, so it was here in his time. Moses Cousins was imprisoned for smuggling in 1833, and appealed to Lord Ilchester for help, following previous unsuccessful appeals to the Vicar and other gentlemen of the village, on the grounds that this was a first offence and that he had been driven to it in a moment of weakness brought about by a life of grinding poverty. The appeal seems to have worked, as he was released 17 days later.

Workshop west of 11 Back Street
and barn adjoining (Whitehill Cottages)

*(Scheduled in the 1974 Village Plan as a building which
the Secretary of State had agreed to include in the statutory list,
with the note that it was "formerly included in the supplementary list")*

Now known as 1-3 Whitehill Cottages, the workshop and barn were rebuilt as cottages by Michael Still, and featured in *Country Life* at the time: they were one of the first new building projects in the village, but not the first project for Michael Still, who had been working as a residential developer since 1973, after 25 years of designing farm buildings. In 1985, he joined forces with architect Clive Hawkings, who worked for him on this development. The *Country Life* feature ended with the words *"if other developers had the same pride that Still has in his work, and the same support from architects, builders and landowners, we might be prouder of what is happening in our villages."* The new cottages are built from Ham stone from the Yeovil area,

The building had been a car mechanic's workshop linked to the garage in West Street before the time of the Appreciation, but it had an earlier life as a cottage if the photograph below is to be believed ~ compare the thatch and window with the distant cottage in the bottom right-hand photograph on p. 22.

(loaned by Dave Stevens)

4 and 6 Back Street

At first sight, these seemed to be the houses referred to in the Parish Council minutes of March 1943, which reported to the powers-that-be that two houses would be needed after the war, and that a site in Back Street had already been chosen. In the event, they turned out to be pre-war ~ the land was purchased by Dorset County Council from the Estate (for 10/- [50p] per house, according to one later conveyance) in October 1938, and building began just before the war with a view to developing six houses. The construction of the other four was interrupted by the war and was never completed. While this pair of houses were occupied during the war ~ literally from the week the war was declared ~ they lacked electricity and the only hot water supply came from coal fire coppers in the kitchens. The building work on this pair was not completed until the war had ended. Though built of brick, according to the present occupant of no. 4, they are bricks which are more than a match for conventional masonry drills.

The pair struck no chord with the author of the Appreciation ~ *"the ghastly semi-detached villas are totally lacking in sympathy with their neighbours. Perhaps the brick work could be colour washed to match the natural stone.'* Well, at least they are half-way there, and it is only fair to remember the austerity years during and after the war, when any house was better than none, though one resident recalls that, although the houses were *"built for local families whose cottages were overcrowded ... there were no takers. Cottages were an average of 1/6 [7.5p] per week as rent."*

9 Back Street

(Listed in the Inventory as "7 and 9 Back Street"
now listed Grade II individually)

Despite the caption in the Appreciation, the photograph is actually of two cottages, no's. 7 and 9, and the outbuilding to no. 9 has been altered and incorporated into the main cottage since 1973. The earlier photograph seems to show some major work being done on no. 7.

7 Back Street

(Listed after 1973 as "barns at rear of 7 and 9 Back Street",
now listed Grade II as "detached cottage, formerly two")

The Appreciation is confusing here: the heading describes the buildings as listed Grade II, while the text has them as unlisted, with a recommendation for Grade II listing. Presumably the author was under the impression that this was itself no. 7 Back Street, and not a set of outbuildings.

5 Back Street

1973

2005

(Grade II listed)

The Appreciation notes ~ *"front covered white and red climbing roses"*. They're still there. Just visible in the background are the outbuildings listed as 7 Back Street, which in fact form part of no. 5. The house is described in the listings register as mid-18th century.

Congregational Church (Studio of Marie Laywine)

1973

2005

(Scheduled in the 1974 Village Plan as a building which the Secretary of State had agreed to include in the statutory list, with the note that it was "formerly included in the supplementary list")

Built by the congregation on land provided by the Estate and with materials donated by the Estate, the Congregational Church was once one of three Free Church buildings in the village. It later became the United Reformed Church, until it was closed in 1977.

A full account of the history of all the nonconformist chapels in Abbotsbury, researched by Peter and Hazel Evans, can be found on the website of the Abbotsbury Heritage Research Project *(www.abbotsbury-heritage.org.uk)*.

After its closure as a church, the building was refurbished for use as a gallery for a wildlife artist, who stayed for only six months, and then it fell into disuse, apart from occasional short-term lettings as a form of saleroom. All the church furniture was taken out in 1977, apart from the chains holding the lights, and a plaque in the porch commemorating a former minister, which occasionally brings in transatlantic visitors tracing their ancestors.

(Below ~ a photograph of the Bible Reading Association's 30th anniversary rally in 1911, in the Congregational Church.)

(loaned by Daphne Sheppard)

3 Back Street

(Scheduled in the 1974 Village Plan as a building which
the Secretary of State had agreed to include in the statutory list)

The house, named in the village plan list as "The Anchorage", was at one time occupied by Don and Norah Burden, but lay empty from 1977, until it was taken over in connection with the studio next door. Given the design of the entrance porch, it may once have been a passage house, i.e. a pair of houses with a single entrance.

It also boasts a segment of the Abbey, the fanged gargoyle high on the left-hand corner of the front wall.

Public Toilets

The cottage which once stood on the site was described as *"long since pulled down"* as far back as 1946. A similar threat appeared to hang over the toilets themselves in 2004, until it emerged that the Council's plans concerned the beach toilets. In fact, the village toilets were totally refurbished in 2005, and a disabled toilet, with a wheelchair ramp, was installed.

The toilets have been here at least since 1968, as the Parish Council asked in that year for direction signs to help visitors, suggesting that the tourist trade was already well established.

At the time of the Appreciation, the toilets earned the dubious distinction of being the only flat-roofed building in the village: *"how someone has tried ! but it is totally out of keeping, the roof a stranger to its neighbours"*. Now it has added to its unfortunate uniqueness with the industrial railings protecting the new ramp: as one villager has commented, *"if any of us applied to put those up, we would have been laughed out of court."*

~ ~ ~ ~ ~ ~

The type K6 telephone kiosk adjoining the toilets was listed Grade II in 1988.

Garages opposite 3 Back Street

Before they were garages, these buildings were apparently stables for the farm based on what was a combination of 2 Back Street and 20 Market Street. According to the 1920s postcard below, the buildings were thatched when they were stables: judging by another postcard from Dave Stevens' collection, the thatch had been replaced by corrugated iron in the late 1930s.

It seems odd that the nearer gable wall appears to be higher than the roofline in the more recent photograph compared to the identical roof in the photograph taken in 1973 ~ unless it is an illusion caused by the thickness of the ivy.

(loaned by Dave Stevens)

2 Back Street and 20 Market Street

(Grade II listed as separate properties, but cross-referenced in the register)

From this angle, there seems to have been no changes, but the 1973 photo shows 20 Market Street as WJ Ferry's shop, selling "Fancy Goods, Postcards, Sweets and Cigarettes", and the 1939 directory lists "Herbert Ferry, china and cards dealer" at this address. The cards came from a huge collection of glass-plate negatives, built up through work for the Estate: some of them were always held at the Estate office, others were used for postcards that were sold by WH Smith until a fire at their printing works destroyed them, and the remainder were acquired by the Estate at a later date. The present occupant's grandmother was a dressmaker skilled enough to work for the Lady Ilchester of the day and teach dressmaking to the village girls.

The Inventory records that both buildings have "re-used ashlar" in the walls ~ a fresh use for Abbey stone ? A middle window on the first floor of 20 Market Street has at some time been blocked up, and a close look at the wall above the left-hand ground floor window implies building work at different times, but the occupant of 20 Market Street believes that this was once a single farm house and bakery which combined these two addresses. Internal evidence in the house supports that belief.

A much earlier photograph from a different viewpoint (below, left), reveals that at one time there was only one window on the Back Street frontage of 2 Back Street: the one on the right of the door had been walled up by then, before being more recently opened up again.

1 Back Street (Old School House Tea Rooms)

(Grade II listed since 1973)

Built originally for the school master in the mid-19th century, and it must have remained the headmaster's house until the school closed in 1981. The 1939 directory shows "HJ Cutler, schoolmaster and Reading Room Secretary" living here.

It was converted from the school master's house into the "Old School House Tea Rooms and Gift Shop" in 1985. Its condition at that time has been described as "gutted", and it seems that it had been divided into two properties (one for the teacher and the other for the policeman, a fearful combination for any miscreant children) before the conversion work began. Mr & Mrs Peach, who carried out the conversion, opened the tea room in 1986, before opening the Oak Room restaurant in Dorchester. The Old School House was then run from 1993 by Mr & Mrs Dawson, who also opened "Abbotsbury Bears & Friends" in Rodden Row in 1995. The Old School House changed hands in 1997, and again in 2002, since when the gift shop has become an extension of the tea room.

The photo below shows how handy the teacher's house was to the school, but also (on the top left, arrowed) the one-time Primitive Methodist Chapel that later became an annexe to the school.

(loaned by Steve Peach)

18 and 16 Market Street

(Grade II listed since 1973)

Built in the mid-19th century Victorian Gothic style of the school across the square, this pair of houses, along with the School House, are the most ornate of the houses built by the Earl of Ilchester in 1858, at the same time as the school itself. The leaded windows are typical of the style, but ~ according to previous owners of the School House ~ are beginning to show their age.

(The left-hand photograph is scanned from the Appreciation text, as the negative is one of the few that could not be found in the files.)

14 Market Street

*(Listed Grade II in 1956 as "terrace 4-14 Market Street"
but now listed individually)*

In the 1973 photograph, the signs in the right-hand ground floor window read "GREGORY, builder and decorator" ~ was this the business based here, or was he simply working on the building ? (According to the present occupants, more likely the latter.) That same window has been replaced since the Appreciation by one that matches the others in the house.

The directory for 1871 lists Emmanuel and Robert Vincent at no. 14 as grocer and shopkeeper (father and son), but by 1875 only Robert is listed, as a market gardener. The directories for 1889 and 1903 then list Joseph Carter as a grocer at no. 14, but by 1939, the house had changed hands, and Thomas Hitchen was listed simply as a shopkeeper here. The shop then passed to Alf White and his wife, who ran it as *"a general store, selling everything from food to paraffin".* It then became a private house.

The roof of the house is unusual for having at least one course of stone slates of the type found more often in the Dordogne than in Dorset. It is described in the listings register as mid-19th century with 20th century windows.

The growth of the tourist trade is reflected in the fact that the direction sign has been moved since 1973 from its original position much nearer the corner of Market Street and Rodden Row so as to give speeding motorists more time to think about using their brakes at the corner. The sign to the "baby swans" (why can't they be called "cygnets" ?) marks the annual hatching celebrations at the Swannery.

12 Market Street

(Grade II listed in 1956 as part of the terrace, but now individually)

Described as late 18th or early 19th century with some refenestration, the house seems virtually unchanged since 1973, apart from the replacement of the left-hand ground floor window with one in the same style as the other windows, an improvement on the earlier facade. The house was re-slated in 2005. For years it was the home of the Gill family who worked on the Abbotsbury branch line.

It also has a strange arrangement on the partition walls ~ on the junction with no. 10, where the cornerstones seem to change their loyalty halfway up the wall, and with no. 14, where the wall seems to be more part of no. 14 than of no. 12.

10 Market Street

8 and 6 Market Street

Grade II listed in 1956 as part of the terrace, but now individually)

(Grade II listed in 1956 as part of the terrace, but now as a pair)

Another 18th century house with 19th century windows. The over-sized right-hand ground floor window betrays the fact that, at one time, this was a shop run by Mr Dunford, the harness-maker. The postcard below (c.1903) shows the shop, as well as the fact that there were once two doors to no. 10. As with no. 12, the window has been changed, though to an 8-pane style compared to the 6-pane style of the others.

The postcard, incidentally, also shows one of Abbotsbury's Victorian street lamps ~ only one surviving standard remains, in the garden of the Abbotsbury Studio in Rodden Row.

Quite a few Abbotsbury shops have become houses, but 6 Market Street is one house that became a shop when the Peach family here brought their business back to the village after a spell in Dorchester, and opened their house as a village version of their Antelope Walk shop.

Other than that, the only change since 1973 is that the fancy hinges to the door of no. 8 have been removed and the door colour changed, but all the evidence suggests that no's. 6 and 8 might originally have been one house ~ there is what looks very like a connecting door between the two, and both the staircase and the inglenook fireplace in no. 8 seem to be fairly recent additions.

Though the pair are described in the listings register as early 19th century, and now have slated roofs, there is evidence in the roof space of no. 6 of a previous thatch, pulled off in a fire c. 1900. Thatch fires have always been a hazard of Abbotsbury life, but that evidence of a thatch tends to imply an earlier date of construction.

(loaned by Dave Stevens)

4 Market Street

(Grade II listed in 1956 as part of the 4-14 Market Street terrace)

The business was run originally by Mr WC Hodder (listed in the 1903 directory and in 1939 as "butcher, retired") ~ the 1900's bill for his purchase is framed in the shop today. Mr Stockley of Portesham worked for Mr Hodder and eventually bought the business from him, taking in as partner a Mr Paye from Weymouth.

It later passed to the Roper family ~ Don Roper was apprenticed butcher in 1936, bought the business in 1961, and his son Colin took it over in 1973. When the shop was refurbished in 2000, an order book for 1910 turned up under the counter, but curiously seemed to deal as much in bread, flour and yeast as in meat.

The business was bought by Rob and Sara Wood in 2001 and renamed "The Village Butcher" ~ the new sign and the changed front door are the only obvious changes to the building.

2 Market Street

(Scheduled in the 1974 Village Plan as a building which the Secretary of State had agreed to include in the statutory list)

The house used to belong to the village butcher, the last one to live here being Mr Hodder. It is described in the Appreciation as an *"unusual house set back from road. Porch and lintols out of character"*. Does that comment have any connection with the thriving wisteria which now covers both the porch and window lintels, but was in its infancy in 1973 ? Back in 1962 when the photograph below was taken, the house was even more unusual, with its rendered facade and utility porch ~ its appearance has improved distinctly since those days, whether 1962 or 1973.

Traffic-watchers will notice that since 1973, the sign giving directions to Weymouth, the Swannery (and in those days, New Barn) has been moved to the far side of the corner and duplicated with one by no. 14 Market Street, while a new sign warning drivers of the corner ahead has also been placed further back up Market Street.

(loaned by Jean Channon)

1 Market Street

(Grade II listed in 1956 and now listed as "Town Farm house and attached rear stables")

Despite the fact that it bears the name "Town Farm", it is described in the Inventory and the 1889 OS map as "Middle Farm". It was formerly two houses with outbuildings behind. Between the houses is a huge chimney serving both sides ~ when it caught fire, the firemen said it was the biggest they had seen.

The Market Street facade was renewed in the 18th century, but the main house was built in the 17th century. Some windows are blocked up and there are large wooden lintels on either side of (and slightly below) the present ground floor windows, and a large opening to the right of the present street door.

The occupant has a theory (which his wife describes as "fantasy") that the big red stones of the frontage are local ironstone and that every six foot along the wall is a slot, which he believes was once the base of a Saxon cruck. The other stones are white ashlar, possibly from Caen, left over once the best Abbey stone had been sold. If the house was Saxon, and the area was a summer retreat for the kings of Wessex, could this once have been home to King Alfred ... ?

The barn behind the house, once a slaughterhouse, was built in 1747. At various times the house has been occupied by different members of families who still live in the village: Abbotsbury people move from house to house as their needs change. When it was a working farm, the garden was an orchard, but an aerial photograph taken in 1924 shows the whole area as allotments ~ even six years after World War I, the pressure to produce food locally was still alive. Although the garden trees appears to be very mature, they were planted after the war by the assistant Head Gardener at the Sub-Tropical Gardens.

Among the mementoes of farm days found by the present occupants were the horses' tails cut off and hung up in their one-time looseboxes, a crucifix and an old Land Girl's pair of jodhpurs.

3 Market Street

(Grade II listed in 1956)

Now part of the adjoining "Flower Bowl", it is used as one of the few holiday cottages in the village, and the door on the right has become a window.

Flowery Bowl tea shop (Post Office)

(Grade II listed in 1956 along with 3 Market Street as a single property)

In late Victorian times according to the trade directories for 1875, 1889 and 1903, this was one of two provisions shops owned by the Ford family, and it specialised in meat and poultry, according to a postcard in Dave Stevens' collection. The family also owned the shop in the square that later became the village Post Office, before the base for village mail moved down to this building. The photograph below is from a late Victorian glass plate taken by an Abbotsbury photographer.

At the time of the Appreciation, though, it had been well established for over a decade as a popular tea room, and was described then as a "pretty little shop front". By the 1990's, it was running as two small shops, here and in no. 3, both building fronts integrated as one, serving teas and selling natural selections, furnishing and goods.

(loaned by Rosemary Rees)

5 Market Street

(Grade II listed in 1956)

The Inventory describes this as a 17th century building with re-used ashlar in the walls, which to me implies the re-use of Abbey stone. Although this whole range of buildings seems to form a unity, a closer look shows that they were all built at different times.

In late Victorian times, this was a bootmaker's shop run by a Mr Gill, and the Reed family lived here for 60 years. At one time, rum was traded from here, according to an account book found during restoration work ~ the existence of an account book may suggest that the trade was a legitimate one. Again, it may not. It was a passage house (a pair of houses with a common entrance): the lobby with two doors is still there.

The "IR SR 1785" plaque above the door suggests the record of a marriage begun here in that year, and may be linked to a story told by an Australian visitor. She had been brought up on the tale of an ancestor working on the 19th century restoration of the parish church, who had fallen in love with a beautiful young girl he had seen sewing in a window and had later married. The house had the name "Bailey" over the door, Unfortunately, there are only a handful of old houses in the village with names over their doors, and when the lady was asked to describe the type of window, it turned out to be a bow window. That presented a fresh problem ~ the only house in the village with a bow window doesn't have a name over the door. The lady's sister in London had apparently done a lot more research on the family's Abbotsbury connections, but has still not come forward with the solution to the mystery.

Unusually, the house is freehold, and may be one of the houses sold for £100 each by the Estate some years ago.

7 Market Street

(Grade II listed in 1956)

It seems a little curious, given that they all seem to be about the same age, that all the houses on the western side of Market Street have dressed stone lintels like this one, while those on the eastern side have a variety of lintels, including brick and timber varieties. The answer may lie in the description of this house as 18th century with 20th century windows. The only other thing that seems to have changed in 30 years is the colour of the front door.

This house was once home to the Daubeney family: Mr Daubeney senior was the landlord of the Ilchester Arms at the time of the first World War, and one of his sons ran Chapel Farm from here. In those days, it was known for the milk churn in the hallway, from which fresh milk was sold.

The Ilchester Arms

(Grade II listed in 1956)

Just visible in the wall is a blocked-up arch, (right) and the marks of the roofline of a building that must once have stood at right angles to the hotel, running outwards into the street: Roger Ross-Turner believes the arch to be pre-Norman, and the building to have been either the market hall or the home of the Guild set up just after the Abbey's foundation.

Edward I gave Abbotsbury a charter for a market in 1271, presumably held in the square, at the head of Market Street. The 1774 edition of Hutchings' History of Dorset refers to *"a very ancient but mean market-house in the middle of town now divided into three tenements",* but the Victorian edition of the book adds the words *"which has since been removed. The site is known by the vulgar appellation of Tal-hal, doubtless a corruption of the Toll hall."* There have been other changes over the years ~ the large arch under the central gable is surely not just decorative, and the keystone to the lintel of one of the ground floor windows is well off-centre.

Was this once the Ship Inn ? A pub of that name features in the 18th century story of Elizabeth Canning, a London girl who claimed to have been kidnapped by a gang whose alibi was that they had been in Abbotsbury at the time, an alibi which was supported by witnesses all the way up (literally) to the Lord Mayor of London, suggesting the importance of the gang to the smuggling business. At any rate, the alibi was good enough to have the original trial verdict overturned.

In March 1808, the Ship was host to a feast for the entire village (around 1000 people) to celebrate the 21st birthday of the then Earl of Ilchester. Queen Victoria is reputed to have visited the inn on a visit to Abbotsbury in 1846, while waiting for her coach wheel to be repaired.

The Ship Inn is listed as such in the 1871 and 1875 trade directories, but the Ilchester Arms appears in the 1889 edition. Tom Cooper, the landlord of the Hotel in Victorian times, wrote, in 1884, one of the earliest guidebooks to Abbotsbury and made sure that readers knew all about his five-star, royalty-patronised establishment.

The coat of arms above the doorway was renovated in 1976 ~ notice that the arms on the gable are not the same as those on the inn sign ~ the arms on the gable are those of Sir Stephen Fox, and those on the sign are the arms of the Fox-Strangways family.

The pub was remodelled in 1984, and again in the late 1990's, when a lot of old furniture and bric-a-brac was removed. It has since changed hands once more, and has returned to looking more like the "Ilch" of old.

"ILCHESTER ARMS"

FAMILY HOTEL,

ABBOTSBURY,

DORSET.

Patronised by T.R.H. Duke and Duchess of Edinburgh.
,, H.R.H. Duke of Connaught.
,, H.S.H. Prince Edward of Saxe Weimar.

This old-established Family Hotel having recently been considerably improved, is now replete with every comfort and accommodation for Visitors. The Hotel is in close proximity with, and commands views of the far famed West Bay and Chesil Beach, St. Catherine's Chapel, the Abbey Ruins, the Earl of Ilchester's splendid Swannery and Semi-Tropical Gardens, all within a short distance of the Hotel.

A Public Dining Room, Drawing Room, Private Sitting Rooms ; cleanly, quiet, and home comforts, with personal attention.

Good Stabling & Lock=up Coach House.

BILLIARDS.

—TARIFF ON APPLICATION.—

T. COOPER, *Proprietor.*

Post Office and 11 Market Street

(Grade III listed at one time, but now Grade II listed)

The main building in this picture ~ 18th century, refashioned early 19th century according to its listing ~ may have been the Post Office at the time of the Appreciation, but the office has moved around the village quite a lot. In the 19th century, it was in the building on the corner of Rodden Row and Market Street, but had moved to this site by 1973, and then in the late 1990's it moved down Market Street some time after the building was changed into two separate shop units, with the Post Office occupying the left-hand half. Two maisonettes were installed on the upper floor as affordable housing in conjunction with the Bournemouth Churches Housing Association and a third flat was built in the back section of the ground floor of the building.

The left-hand half was converted from the re-styled Post Office in April 2000 into a picture framing business and gallery run by three local artists who had previously run successful exhibitions in Langton Herring and in the Strangways Hall here. In 2002, the gallery changed hands but continued in the same field of work, changing hands yet again in 2005, and now operates under the title "d'Veitch Art Gallery".

The right-hand half was opened as a take-away food shop, changing hands and becoming a tearoom in 2002, and once more changing hands in 2003 and yet again in 2005.

13, 15 and 17 Market Street

(Grade II listed in 1956 as a pair, but now listed as three houses)

Described as *"typical Industrial Revolution Cottages"*, this trio was built in 1841 for Estate employees. The photographs show much more of no's. 15 and 17 than they do of no. 13, which may be an older property than the other two ~ the stone work appears older, the windows are at different levels, and there is a dividing line between no. 13 and no. 15.

No. 13 doubles up as a gallery and workshop as well as a family house, modernised in 1963 ~ the business side showcases jewellery and works in felt, as well as website design and search engine optimisation. The house was once two cottages, the back one a ruin until the 1980's, when it was incorporated into the front part. What is now the gallery was once presumably a stable, and there is evidence of other buildings behind, including the former privy, now a garden shed.

No. 15 was one of nine properties sold in 1922 when (according to local legend) the highways authority refused to improve the B3157 through the village on the grounds that the Ilchester Estate owned all the houses fronting the road. The house remained in the ownership of the Cribb family until 1970, when it was sold to a Mr Pendrill, and on his death it passed to his wife, who was a teacher in the Abbotsbury school, and remarried to become Mrs Snow. The Snows extended the house in 1986, nearly doubling its size and adding garages off Chapel Lane. The house was once more sold, in 1992, and yet again, to Leon and June Edwardes, in 1994. Throughout all these changes, the original downstairs back window was left in place, with etchings of a milkmaid and a cow on one of the window panes.

No. 17 is home to a leading figure in the Abbotsbury Cricket Club, founded nearly 150 years ago, which won the 2005 Wisden award for the most beautiful cricket ground in the country.

19 Market Street (Fleet Cottage)

(Grade II listed in 1956)

The Inventory describes the house as *"having original 17th-century stone-mullioned windows and a doorway with a four-centred head"*. The Appreciation calls it *"delightful"*, then spoils the effect by adding *"link to barn ... out of character, spoils charming rear elevation"*. He is, of course, talking about the barn (overleaf) that is now Chapel Lane Stores, and not casting any aspersions on this house or its outbuildings. The author tries to redeem the faux pas by noting the *"rear splendid windows in thatch"*, but didn't notice the "salt box", the part of the building that was used to salt down the fish that were once caught in their thousands off Chesil Beach.

The thatch has been renewed several times since the Appreciation photograph, when it certainly seemed to be in need of a new "haircut". Apparently the life expectancy of Abbotsbury thatch depends as much on the activities of the local birds as it does on the climate and the skill of the thatcher.

Barn next to 19 Market Street (Chapel Lane Stores)

(Recommended in the Appreciation for Grade II listing)

Chapel Lane Stores has to be one of the more dramatic "change-of-use" planning permissions in recent years. At the time of the Appreciation, it was a net store and loggers' workshop: in the summer, the Arnold family (the last of the many fishing crews that once worked commercially at mackerel fishing) stored the nets they used in seine fishing off Chesil Beach, a process described in *"The Seiners and the Knocker Up".*

At the end of the fishing season in October or November, the business turned over to logging, with a large circular saw in the middle of the building and a kindling store in the far corner. It wasn't until 1994 that it was turned into the present busy general stores, a shop that is not only "open all hours" but has become ever more versatile over the years, adding a video library, daily and weekly newspapers, and a hole-in-the-wall cash machine to its services. In 2005, the owners sold on the business for a well-earned semi-retirement.

Yet there is a precedent for businesses here in this lane. The directory for 1871 lists Joseph Symes the tailor and John Walls the bootmaker operating from Chapel Lane. The tailor was still there when the 1875 directory was published, and the directories for 1889 and 1903 both list Joseph John Limm as a shopkeeper in Chapel Lane ~ but the 1889 Ordnance Survey map doesn't show the cottages that once stood at right angles to Chapel Lane, near the present garages. Only the photo, right, from Dave Stevens' collection, records their existence.

(loaned by Dave Stevens)

22 to 28 Market Street

(Unlisted in 1973, but now Grade II listed as 4 estate cottages built 'en bloc')

The Appreciation points out that only around the square are gable ends turned towards the street, here on these cottages, on the school and the Ilchester Arms. Abbotsbury houses butt right on to the pavement: very few of them have front gardens, and those that do always date from the 19th century.

On the wall in front of no. 22 is the letter "P", denoting that this was once the village's police house, before the policeman was moved to Linton Cottage on the outskirts of the village.

This was where the 1954 Garland Day procession was halted by the village bobby. Every year, on 13th May, the children of the village have, for centuries, carried garlands of flowers around the village before taking them down to the beach, where the garlands would be loaded on to the fishing boats and cast adrift at sea to ensure a good harvest. In the days when the school was next door to these houses, Garland Day was a holiday; and it was celebrated on the 13th, because that would have been May Day if the calendar had not been changed in the 18th century, losing 11 days in the process and causing public riots at the time. (Alternative theories on the origin of Garland Days here and elsewhere link them to Royalist sympathies and a connection with Oak Apple Day.)

In 1954, the local policeman decided that the pennies collected by the children constituted begging, and he impounded the garlands ~ and the children carrying them. The furious mothers complained to the Parish Council, and the Honourable John Strangways took the matter up. The children were released, the policeman was reprimanded, and the Chief Constable even apologised. Since then, nobody has dared meddle with Garland Day: the problem now is to keep the custom alive.

School (Strangways Hall)

1973

2005

(Unlisted in 1973, but now Grade II listed)

This School was erected by the Earl of Ilchester in 1858, after the earlier "school house" was burnt down, along with several other houses. Old photographs show a bell tower in the centre of the school roof. It was removed on safety grounds many years ago ~ so far, village memories have been unable to come up with a precise date.

The school had been originally endowed in 1758 by the Earl's ancestor, Mrs Strangways Horner, when she also donated a building for the school and its master. The Ilchester ladies seem to have taken a strong interest in the school: the old logbooks record regular visits, and in 1874, Lady Ilchester gave 24 print dresses to the most regular attenders, and sent down 12 dusters and 24 kitchen rubbers to be hemmed and marked. In the following year, she gave 12 pairs of boots to the most regular attenders among the boys. The vicar was not so supportive ~ the Revd Mr Penny complained that 55-70 boys had been bowling and dancing at the Ship Inn during Abbotsbury Fair, and added that if Lord Ilchester didn't stop the bowling and dancing, he (the vicar) would never enter the school again.

It must have been a pretty spartan school: the logs report constant problems of attendance, due to the heating and condition of the building, and as recently as 1946, the village youth group were asking for electric lighting, leading the Parish Council to ask why there was none installed. (When electricity cables were installed for the village in the late 1940's, a 30-feet deep well was uncovered in the square in front of the school.) New heating and lighting were not, in fact, put in until the school became the village hall, with the hope that the WI could be persuaded to move home from the Reading Room in Rodden Row.

The school closed in 1981, after a vigorous campaign fought by parents and the Parish Council from 1973, and the Estate bought the building back from the County Council in 1982.

Edward Green, the Estate manager at the time, commented on the irony of the fact that the Strangways family had built the original school in 1758, put up the new building in 1858, sold it to the Council for £2,000 in 1920, and were now buying it back again, adding that the sum paid *"represents a considerable return to the Council on its initial outlay"*, as the Estate had to pay the full residential market value, the Council having sought planning permission for housing on the site.

The one-time school became the Strangways Hall in 1985 and was given to the village in return for an annual rent of a bouquet of flowers, and the condition that the Strangways name be remembered in the hall's title. As a hall, it became so popular with so many village groups (and several from farther afield) that bookings had to be made weeks in advance, but in 2001, dry rot was discovered under the toilets, and expensive repairs had to be taken on. A group of ladies stitched a 42-panel quilt which was raffled over the summer of 2002, raising £1,200 towards the cost of repairs. The quilt was won by a therapist from Blandford, who took it as a sign that she should go ahead with her dream of building her own treatment room, and it now hangs there to soothe her cancer patients. A group of four dozen people have now been meeting weekly in the hall to stitch a dramatic "crazy patchwork" cover for the grand piano in the parish church.

Meanwhile, children are now back in the school building, which houses the Chesil Bank Pre-School: a rather different type of child, and a very different type of schooling from their 19th-century predecessors below ~ the date on the boy's slate appears to read "National School, Abbotsbury, 1872".

(loaned by Daphne Sheppard)

1,3 and 5 Church Street

(Grade II listed in 1956)

Described in the Appreciation as a *"neat terrace of Industrial Revolution Cottages"*, but the description is let down by the comment *"view through gate of general muddle with 2 garden sheds and Church behind"*.

No. 1 was once home to Mr & Mrs Stokes: he was one of two butchers in the village, working from a shed in Back Street, with a slaughter house on higher ground at the top of Rosemary Lane. He was followed by Mr and Mrs Maurice Ford, who moved out in 1971 when the house was comprehensively modernised by the provision of a bathroom and kitchen, and a tidier arrangement for the area behind the cottages, which had previously all had separate yards with steps to the top pathway.

Meanwhile, no. 5 became the new home for Mabel Claxton when her house in Rosemary Lane became uninhabitable ~ see p. 19.

Old Manor House

(Grade II listed in 1956 and now listed as Grade II)*

The Conservation Plan describes the Manor House as *"a post-medieval building with gable stacks to which have been added 17th, 18th, 19th and 20th century extensions."* One of the authors adds that *"the southern wing - or at least all its architectural detailing - is suspiciously pristine, and the facework displays an apparently deliberate mix of sharp irregular rubble blocks. If not wholly invented in the 19th or early 20th century, this wing must have been extensively worked over in the 1943 and later works to the extent that none of the architectural detailing is more than 100 years old."* The Inventory, however, says that the front block and the north-west wing are late 18th century, while the south-west wing (on the extreme left of the photos) is 17th century. Originally the whole roof was covered with roofing stone (as remains now only on the porch) until the pre-18th century roof structure was replaced. The dormer windows have been replaced and modified since the 1973 photograph.

The Old Manor House served as a vicarage according to Dorset trade directories from 1903 to 1939. At one time divided into two separate houses, it later became the home for the eldest son of the Earl of Ilchester at the time ~ the Honourable John Fox Strangways (known to the village as "the Hon John"), and later for the Honourable Mrs Townshend, the current head of the Ilchester Estate and still known to the village as "Miss Charlotte". One of the improvements she made to the house was to add a tennis court, completed in 3 months, despite being carved out of quite steeply sloping ground, and to lay out the formal gardens. Since 1991, the Manor House has been let to private tenants.

Old Vicarage

(Grade II listed in 1956)

Surgery Market Street

According to the Dorset trade directory for 1903, this was then the doctor's house, and it served as such for many years, which is no doubt why the smaller building next door was his surgery until very recent times. Not immediately obvious to passers-by is the 14th century blanked-off window in the flank wall adjoining the Manor House, a feature which seems to be at odds with the listing description of the house as early 19th century.

The rendering around some of the windows has apparently been broken open to establish if a case can be made for gaining listed building consent to remove all the cement rendering from the frontage of the house and restore it to the original stone facade.

It carries the name of a vicarage because it was occupied by the village vicars after the last resident doctor left. The last resident vicar here was the Revd Canon Ball, formerly Chaplain to HM Prison on Dartmoor, who moved to the new vicarage (p. 7) in 1964, since when the Old Vicarage has been a private house.

A very convenient health centre for Abbotsbury folk, until the demands of economy and NHS regulations forced its closure in favour of a purpose-built health centre in Portesham. (The same demanding requirements later closed the Bride Valley surgery, centralising all medical services from then on in Portesham.)

The building has changed little since 1973, despite the best efforts of unskilled lorry drivers ~ but the signage on the gable wall has grown apace.

1 to 4 Red Lane

(Grade III listed in 1973 and now Grade II listed ~ 1 and 2 as a pair, with 3 and 4 as a separate pair)

All four cottages are described as 18th century buildings.

The 1889 OS map shows a "Methodist Chapel (Primitive)" behind the school, and approached by a lane to the right of these cottages. It's still there, having spent its latter days as an extension to the School, but fell victim to a fire while used as a store after the School had moved to Portesham. The Appreciation describes a *"stone cobbled pavement"* to West Street, but unfortunately most of that disappeared under a mixture of tarmac and gravel in the 1990s. Oddly, the Appreciation thought *"how nice it would be to open up the area of grass behind the railings in front of these cottages"*, but if it had been opened up, and the suggested new house had been built behind the village green, the safe area where today's small children kick footballs around would have gone.

The lane is called "Red Lane" after the iron ore in the soil at the head of the lane, and the DIGS (Dorset Important Geological Sites) Group have marked it out as geologically significant. The iron was one of the reasons for bringing a railway to the village, but there was never enough of the stuff to make the line commercially viable. Local knowledge has it, though, that mortar for repointing local walls should be mixed with a little soil from Red Lane to produce just the right colour to blend with the local stone.

5 Red Lane and barn adjoining

(Unlisted in 1973, but now Grade II listed)

The only obvious change here is that the "barn adjoining" has been incorporated into no. 5. At one time it belonged to the branch of the Ford family who ran what later became the Post Office next door to the Ilchester Arms (the precision is needed to distinguish it from the various other Post Offices that have existed in the village). In those days, the *"barn adjoining"* was indeed a barn and store room, complete with a projecting beam and pulley for hoisting stores into the upper floor. The barn later became a garage before being turned into extra accommodation for no. 5, and the garage beyond the barn also belonged to the Ford family shop.

The house itself, described as mid-19th century in contrast to the other Red Lane properties, was modernised many years ago, but when it was first returned to private ownership after being used as a wartime Army billet, it consisted essentially of one room, with the water supply coming from a tap in the lane. The modernisation included removing cupboards from either side of a fireplace, to reveal an ingle nook extending nearly the entire depth of the front room.

Barn at end of Red Lane

50 West Street

(Grade II listed in 1956)

Now you see it, now you don't. It's difficult to know where a building as temporary as this ever stood, but people with longer memories of the village than mine assure me that this was about the right spot, on the left hand side near the top of Red Lane. It's not surprising it has gone ~ the roof was corrugated iron, the doors were plywood, and the walls were a mixture of rubble and breeze block. The author of the Appreciation sensitively said only that it *"should be refaced if possible".*

The area beyond it has been levelled out over the years, and there is some local scepticism about the belief that it was once ever a quarry for iron ore.

A pre-1914 postcard in Dave Stevens' collection shows that the 1973 glass porch replaced an earlier enclosed timber porch to the house, and reveals that in those days it was known as "Cotoneasters". Descriptions in the listings register once related a large part of West Street to this house ~ e.g. *"one of a range of cottages west of Cotoneaster".* A puzzling feature of the house is the set of shallow keystoned arches set into the stonework above the door and ground floor windows and above the string course: the sash windows seem original. The Appreciation describes the house as *"untypical house but mellowed".* Thirty years, and the removal of the rendering has mellowed it even more.

In the early 1980s and before, it was occupied by Peter Blackmore, screenplay writer for many of the Norman Wisdom comedies. The house was next occupied by a local farmer and his wife. The milk churns in the left-hand photo would have been an everyday site even as recently as 1973 ~ now they appear mainly in antique shops.

49 West Street

(Grade II listed in 1956)

This was at one time a "passage house" ~ the street door opened into a lobby with a door off on either side leading to two separate houses. For some reason, that type of house seemed to be largely confined to the western half of the village. The adjoining wall has always enclosed the garden, not to this house but to no. 50, and is not the remnant of a previous house frontage.

It is listed as an "attached cottage", mid-19th century, formerly three houses, which suggests that the cannon ball found here and now serving as a doorstop in the Abbotsbury Pictures gallery was perhaps not a stray shot that landed here, but might have been brought to this house some time after the Civil War stormed through Abbotsbury.

48 West Street

(Grade II listed in 1956 as "part of four cottages west of Cotoneaster")

According to the present occupant, this might once have been called "Withy Cottage". It has a plaque over the door bearing the inscription "1764 ML ME".

The low wall on the left is the frontage of a now extinct house ~ the Inventory describes it as early 18th century, implying that it was still standing when the Inventory was published in 1952. According to the Appreciation, *"No.47 missing remains front and rear walls now form yard between 47* (sic) *and 48. Could possibly be rebuilt."* The fact that the house numbering, done in the 1950s, allowed for a no. 47 to be rebuilt again suggests that enough of it stood then to justify its inclusion ~ certainly enough of it remained in the early 1970's for a village youngster to break his leg there while trying to climb the ruined chimney. The photograph below proves that a complete house (arrowed) stood there in pre-war years. A better photograph of the house is on p. 66.

West Street house numbering is unusual ~ the numbers run in sequence 1-16 westwards along one side of the street, while numbers 17-50 run eastwards along the other side: the rest of the village follows the normal convention of odd numbers on one side and even ones on the other. That's why, over the next few pages, the numbers keep dropping and don't start to rise again until you reach p. 53.

(loaned by Dave Stevens)

44, 45, 46 West Street

(Grade II listed in 1956 as "one of a range of cottages West of Cotoneaster")

These houses are virtually unchanged since the photo taken for the Appreciation, apart from the door colours, and the double yellow lines in the road. Even the TV aerials were there thirty years ago.

Shop, 43 West Street

(Grade II listed in 1956 in the same terms as no's 44-46)

The Virgina creeper has returned! A 1904 postcard in Dave Stevens' collection shows the plant moving upwards and outwards from the front door: by the 1912 postcard in the same collection, it had reached the eaves and was advancing on the shop window. At the time of the Appreciation, it had been cut back, but as the right-hand photo shows, it seems to have come back ~ "seems", because this is a fresh planting, but is no less vigorous for all that.

This was once a shop run by the Toms family (Samuel Toms, baker, features in the 1903 directory, and Tom Toms, also a baker, appears in the 1939 edition), and then by George and Pat Hawes at the time of the Appreciation, and was in business as recently as 1981. It is now a private house.

Only visible when the leaves fall from the creeper in winter are some carved faces in the wall ~ Abbey, perhaps, but they look rather too modern for that.

Barn at rear of 43 West Street

The author of the Appreciation took his brief to list every Abbotsbury building seriously enough to include this barn, perhaps because he thought the "Hampshire hipped ends" to the slated part of the roof worth a mention.

40, 41, 42 West Street

1973

2005

38, 39 West Street

1973

2005

This trio of late Victorian houses and the pair next door (all apparently built in 1891) appear on a pre-1920's postcard in the Dave Stevens collection. The two gardens were once heavily cultivated. The Appreciation has a low opinion of them, saying that they *"look massive and out of proportion"*, that the group *"tower over the road"*, that the *"gables and bulk (are) out of character"* and that the street scene here *"tends to break down"*. Maybe, but they must have some fine views of Chapel Hill.

The Estate did some major in-house refurbishment to no. 41 in 2004, won planning permission to erect some new houses on ground to the east (just off the right hand side of these photos) and began building work in the summer of 2005. At least the new houses will not, if the preliminary diggings are any guide, be quite so high above road level as their neighbours, and may even succeed in linking two rooflines that are at quite different heights. The extent of the success can be gathered from the entry on p. 91.

The houses are unusual in that the normal entrances to all of them are at the back, opposite a range of outbuildings not visible from the road, and it is interesting to see how the architect has managed to make the trio look so like the pair next door ~ only the position of the chimneys and the placing of the central ground-floor window spoils the passing illusion that these are an identical pair of semis.

As already mentioned, these houses and those next door appear on a pre-1920's postcard in the Dave Stevens collection: an unusual card in that it avoids the clichéd Abbotsbury views. Again, the main entrance to these houses is at the back.

36 and 37 West Street and building adjoining

(The whole terrace of six cottages (32 to 37) were listed Grade II in 1956)

In 1935, the District Surveyor was asked to remove the steps here ~ they are still here (despite a further request in 1963), because the Parish Council was told that it would be held responsible for any accident caused by their removal.

A couple of sculptors live in no. 36 and the "building adjoining" ~ their work includes the restoration of the fountain in the courtyard of Linlithgow Palace in Scotland, a Portland stone memorial bench on Chapel Hill, and a lettered Portland plaque for Wheelwrights in Rodden Row.

The major change between these two photographs is not in the houses, but in the trees that now tower over them. Presumably the work going on in the earlier photograph was part of the general modernisation that coincided with the Appreciation.

35 and 35a West Street and building adjoining

(The whole terrace of six cottages (32 to 37) were listed Grade II in 1956)

These two cottages were the subject of major restoration in 1973, described in detail in the Appreciation. Before then, they had lain derelict since the last tenant, a Mrs Limm, left in the late 1960's. One of the cottages won some notoriety in 1956, when the tenant asked the Parish Council why a council house in Hands Lane had been vacated and re-let when she had been told she was first on the waiting list: it emerged that the allocation had been made by RDC officers without consulting the local councillor or the housing sub-committee.

At the time of the restoration, the eastern end of no. 35a was a spar-maker's workshop with an earth floor, and the rest of the building, described as a "hovel", had been condemned. The numbering is confusing, as the house had been divided into two flats, one upstairs and one downstairs, but has always been known as "35a" ~ the door which somebody thought led to no. 35 actually opens to a passage way.

Mr Lockton, who had commissioned the restoration, only lived in the house for four years ~ he didn't get the space he had hoped for, because he was only permitted to add a single-storey extension to the back of the house. It is not really a family house: the two bedrooms are widely separated, and the ground floor is perhaps too "open plan" for a family with children.

All the same, the restoration is imaginative, and the internal walls are positively crammed with decorative stones which must have come from the Abbey, including what might be a stoup, set in vertically to one wall ~ and a mummified cat in a tiny recess (overleaf), bearing witness to older beliefs. The actual building work was carried out by Roger Ross-Turner and Peter Reid, with carpentry by Cyril Toms, who carved his name and the date into the stairs he built.

(continued overleaf)

When Mr Toms came back many years later for further work on the house, he was surprised to find that the wood had not moved in any way. Mr Lockton's survey on the house claimed that parts of it were 13th century: when work was under way on the walls, one of them neared collapse, and had to be carefully dismantled, every stone numbered, and replaced in exactly the original position.

The house was acquired with funding from a family will, and the purchase was completed in November 1977 on the anniversary of the benefactor's birth. After being used for "weekending" for a few years, it became a permanent home in 1981.

It is described in the listings register as 17th century with an earlier core.

The mummified cat lurking in its recess.

(A similar cat still lies in the roof space at Abbey House ~ brought down prior to disposal during restoration work there, it brought nothing but bad luck until it was put back in its rightful home.)

32 to 34 West Street

(The whole terrace of six cottages (32 to 37) were listed Grade II in 1956)

The former reference point for the terrace changed here ~ no longer cottages *"West of Cotoneaster"*, they were described in 1956 as *"part of six cottages adjoining Rose Cottage"*.

No. 32 has known an extraordinary sequence of uses since 1973, when it looked as if it was just another cottage. In the 1990's it was a surgery for the local vet, then for a time it became an office for part of the Abbotsbury Software team before passing in to the hands of a rival computer firm. In its latest form, it has become the office for an educational charity, though it was unoccupied at the time the right-hand photograph was taken in the spring of 2004.

No's. 33 and 34 are at least 300 years old, for they were rebuilt after a fire in 1704. They are described in the Appreciation as a pottery: a new kiln was installed in 1973 for the pottery opened in 1956 by Roger Ross Turner (popularly known as "Gillie" after the wartime radio comedian Gillie Potter) and his son Jason, then a student at Camberwell and now living in America. The kiln had to be craned over the thatched roof, and the roof removed from the workshop. The pottery was later taken over by Roger Gilding, and the last of the pottery equipment was only removed in 2005.

Roger Ross-Turner senior died in the early 1960's, aged 78. By all accounts he was a character, driving everywhere in an A40 van; one of his works was a large cockerel made for the boardroom of Courage's brewery in the days when there were no less than 97 pubs in Weymouth.

The building is now home to Abbotsbury Pictures, a framing service and art gallery. The photograph was taken during Dorset Art Week in 2004, and the gallery is liberally festooned with DAW banners and posters.

30 and 31 West Street

(The two houses were listed Grade II as a pair in 1956)

The Appreciation comments that these two houses are *"probably not so old'* as no's. 32-35, with *"obviously higher rooms and better built than 32-35"*. Both of them have been modernised to a degree, and no. 31 was originally one of the many "passage houses" in the village, with the street door opening into a wide lobby which led to two separate front doors. In those days, each of the two houses had a single room downstairs and two first-floor bedrooms. Here at least the passage only gave entrance to the cottage either side ~ further along West Street a passage apparently also served as a right of way to the hillside behind.

Barn next to 30 West Street

(Scheduled in the 1974 Village Plan as a building which the Secretary of State had agreed to include in the statutory list)

Appearing in the 1974 Village Plan list as a workshop, this little building has seen a few changes in more recent years.

In the late 1990's, it was the shop and workshop for Iris Way, who moved from her base at the Flower Bowl in Market Street, where she made and sold colourful cushions and exotic waistcoats, and ran a clothes alteration service, before deciding to work direct from home.

At that point it became "Abbotsbury Antiques", a *brocante* run as a retirement hobby, selling all sorts of things ~ the bicycle on the pavement is actually a sale item, but could equally have provided healthy transport home for the shop owner, who lives little more than a hundred yards away.

Buildings behind barn

(Grade II listed as "Water Outlet with arch-surround")

It is not clear why the description in the Appreciation refers initially to buildings which are not visible from the street, and are not featured in the photograph, especially as there was apparently never any barn here. The description goes on to describe the fountain head as a *"central arched niche with lion's head. 1859 plaque. Water outlet appears to be of medieval origin"*.

In the Village Plan of 1974, it appears on the supplementary list of *"other buildings which the Secretary of State has agreed to include in the statutory list when it is revised"* as a stone arch on the boundary wall on the north side of West Street. It would seem that the agreement has been honoured.

29 West Street

(Grade II listed in 1956 as a detached cottage with a converted outbuilding at the west end)

The main changes to this building (described in the listing register as 18th century rebuilding with 20th century renovation) are that the door on the left has been replaced with a window to match its neighbours and that two new ground floor windows have been inserted in the gable wall by the new gateway.

The angle bracket in the front wall, to the right of the wall-tie in the right-hand photograph is one of 40-odd "scabbards" on Abbotsbury buildings, put there to house Christmas trees which are placed around the village as part of the "Abbotsbury Noel" festivities which were first celebrated in the late 1990's.

25 to 28 West Street and storage building

1973

2005

(Most of the terrace was Grade II listed in 1956, apart from the "storage building" on the left, which the author of the Appreciation thought "might be included with listed buildings".)

All five houses, previously described as "virtually derelict", were completely rebuilt in 1982 by Kerslake and Wakefield of Winterbourne Steepleton to designs by Yeovil architect NJ Hitchcox, and the cottages were put on leasehold sale in 1983 ~ the centre ones at £27,500, the west end one at £32,500 and the east end cottage, larger than the others (thanks to a two-storey extension unlike the single-storey rear additions to the others), at £35,000. (A contemporary newspaper cutting quotes higher intended prices, so the market may have been sluggish, or the cottages ~ it has been said ~ didn't appeal to local folk.) One of the present occupants has a Victorian photograph of the terrace, with little girls in pinafores on one side of the road, and an open culvert on the other. In between is a road that is a lot less well surfaced than the present B3157. That, and the brick-built privy at the top of the steep rear garden, reminds one of just how far Abbotsbury has improved since "the old days".

The rebuilding was, according to one local resident, almost total, with virtually only the front facade left intact, rather alarming the neighbours, who feared the collapse of the wall during the stormy weather at the time. Prior to the work, the gardens were all open to the back, as there was a right of way across the top of the gardens to give rear access to the cottages, but the need for parking space has closed them off, and they all became smaller when the rebuilding work involved the creation of single-storey extensions at the back of each cottage, and the creation of a new house, no.25a at the western end of the terrace.

The 1939 directory lists James Fuzzard as a carpenter in West Street, presumably working out of no.25, where the white double doors seem to have been the entrance to a workshop. Was he also the "champion potato grower" whose efforts appear in a postcard in Dave Stevens' collection ?

23 and 24 West Street

1973

2005

(Grade II listed in 1956)

Unusually for the village, this pair of cottages is at right angles to the main road, implying that at the time they were built, Cowards Lane was a more important lane than it is now.

Apart from the obvious changes, such as the two windows that have been inserted into the West Street gable end of no. 24, and the tiny light that has been opened up on its main frontage, there are in no. 23 what the Appreciation calls "alien components", namely the fact that *"openings have concealed steel lintols with rubble stone continued over without any external arches or lintols and standard wooden windows with hopper lights."* Perhaps this is another example of what was happening in Abbotsbury before it won conservation area status. This is yet another house that has been home to more than one village family at different times in its life, once being the first home for a former village butcher and his new wife.

The photo (below), taken from the Appreciation, shows the view up the lane leading to *"a pleasantly proportioned dilapidated slate roofed building ... almost hidden from view behind overgrown shrubbery"*. The author of the Appreciation hoped that it might be repaired and put to some use, but the one-time stable or piggery had gone soon after that, and a double garage was built on its site in 2000.

21 and 22 West Street

(Grade II listed as "19 and 22 [formerly listed as cottage on West of Cowards Lane]")

Some real changes here, or so it appears.   The 1973 photograph implies, perhaps because of the doorway, that the main house here is no. 21, possibly a passage house, and that no. 22 is the right-hand half of the pair, entered by the same doorway.   The present occupant of no. 22 says that it is frequently addressed as "21/22 West Street".   The reality is that no. 22 has always faced on to Coward's Lane, and is entered by crossing Coward's Lake, the little stream that comes down from the ridge and crosses under West Street before resurfacing alongside no. 13 (p. 55).   Meanwhile, the door in the 1973 photograph has been turned into a window, and the one-time no. 21 has been absorbed into the houses on either side.

21, 20, 19 and 18 West Street

No. 18 in 1973   No. 19 in 1973   No. 20 in 1973   No 21 in 1973, (with part of 22)

1973

2005

(Scheduled for listing in 1974 draft Village Plan)

Though it might not seem so at a quick glance, this little terrace has probably been changed as much as (if not more than) many other Abbotsbury cottages. The upper pictures make it clear that there were four individual cottages here in 1973, but today's map of the village shows only three, and one of these (no. 22) has turned its back on the other two.

The doors to the former no's. 19 and 21 have gone, to be replaced by windows, yet the old door to no. 20 remains, even if it now bears the number "19". The one-time no. 19 is also unique in having the only householder to appear in any of the Appreciation photographs ~ seven cars, one workman, this lady, and a horse, in 147 photographs of what seems to be an otherwise totally deserted village. It couldn't be done now.

Only no. 18 retains its identity, even if it has, like the one-time no. 19, lost its block-marked rendered wall.   Quite why they were treated in that way is anybody's guess, especially as they are almost the first houses the visitor sees on entering Abbotsbury from the west: once again, it couldn't be done now.

17 West Street

1973 **2005**

16 West Street

(Grade II listed in 1956 as "single cottage, formerly two attached cottages")

The first house in the village, (unless you count West Lodge, p. 91) standing back, as that one does, from the main road. At the time of the Appreciation, it looked as if it ought to be a pair of cottages, but is only numbered as one house, and it no longer has the western porch.

This is the point where the numbering crosses the road to head back into the village. That idiosyncratic West Street numbering forced the author of the Appreciation to list houses in a way that makes sense on the ground, but reads back-to-front in the book. So far, the photographer has been working west from the village centre along the north side of West Street. The next house has him returning to the village centre along the south side of the street, so that, having started with no. 50, he ends with no. 1.

Here we start on the south side of West Street, and the numbers are still decreasing. One of several houses that have acquired bits of decorative Abbey stonework ~ the Appreciation notes that this one has *"moulded stone from Abbey over door"*. The listings register describes it as 18th century with newer windows.

No 16 was home to the Toms family from c. 1936 until c. 1983. Mr Toms was an Estate carpenter, a boat builder at Wyke Regis during World War II, a fisherman, and served as a volunteer night watchman at Coastguards.

In 1958, the District Surveyor was asked to do something about the water on the road here *"as passing traffic splashed the water 4ft high and if the front door was open, water went right through it"*. This stretch of road is still vulnerable to traffic entering the village at excessive speeds, unaware of quite how narrow the carriageway is about to become.

The house was for many years linked to an orchard and market garden (now the site of West Lodge, described on p. 91), until it was modernised in 1983, together with the adjoining building, by Maureen and Peter Bowring, the then landlords of the Ilchester Arms, who had acquired a lease from the Estate. The Bowrings gained planning permission to create the present cottage from no. 16 and the store described as "Next to 16", provided the frontage was not altered. The only later addition to the house has been an artist's studio, added to the garage at the rear of the garden in 1998.

Next to 16 West Street

(Grade II listed in 1956)

Another house with bits of decorative Abbey stonework ~ the Appreciation notes though, that this one has *"part old moulding stone from Monastry (sic) over door"* and *"old limestone quoins to doorway"*. A curious comment, when so many houses have dressed stone that looks to the layman suspiciously like limestone.

At one time a warehouse, it became a part of no. 16 next door when the latter was modernised in 1983. Now listed with no. 16, it was formerly listed as *"part of cottages west of Cowards Lane"*.

14 and 15 West Street

(Scheduled in the 1974 Village Plan as a building which the Secretary of State had agreed to include in the statutory list)

No. 14 appears in that Village Plan list without its neighbour no. 15, which seems a curious omission ~ despite all appearances to the contrary, they are two separate houses. The frontage to the narrow road is deliberately rather bare, as the houses are designed to look south across to Chapel Hill.

Barn next to 13 West Street

(Grade II listed as part of no. 13)

Described in the Appreciation as a *"single storey barn"* and having windows *"in west flank high level loft with wood shutters"*. The barn is in the process of being incorporated into no. 13 itself and converted to residential use. It contains, like other village cottages, a fair selection of stones that have found their way from the Abbey.

13 West Street

1973 **2005**

(Grade II listed)

The Appreciation comments on the *"stone lintols with central keystone"*. It also contains a selection of decorated Abbey stone throughout the house.

Ernest Ford, smallholder, was entered in the 1939 directory at this address.

The house is now called "Cowards Lake" after the stream which flows alongside it from the Ridgeway down to the sea. "Lake" is apparently the Saxon word for a slow-flowing stream, and not a confusion with Cowards Lane across the road, but given the gradient involved, "slow-flowing" is not always an accurate term.

12 West Street (Chesil House)

1973　　　　　　　　　　**2005**

The author of the Appreciation clearly didn't like this house, including it in *"things which mar the scene"* ~ *"its blue painted windows and hipped roof ... jars."* At the time it was built, though, it must have been considered (at least by the man who commissioned it and the architect who designed it) the height of fashion, and conservation was not as widely rated as it is today. It stands on the site of a terrace of small thatched cottages that all perished in the famous Abbotsbury blaze of 1704.

According to the present occupants, it was built in 1925 as a house for the Estate Manager, at the same time as Linton Cottage (p. 70) was built as a police house. It was later home to one of the family from New Barn Farm who moved into the village itself, here and at 13 Rodden Row. In the 1939 directory, George White, motor car proprietor, appears at this address, named as "Homeleigh" ~ it is now called "Chesil House" after a spell as "Chesil Cottage", an inappropriate name for a substantial house.

11 West Street with barn and link

1973　　　　　　　　　　**2005**

(Grade II listed as "no. 11 with attached building")

The Appreciation recommended that no. 11 and the "link" (which was incorporated into no. 11 between 1974 and 1977), should be listed, and notes the tiled roof on no. 11, an unusual feature in the older village houses. The open area on the right of the earlier photograph is now occupied by Chestnut Cottage (p. 89).

The 1939 directory lists Charles Ford, market gardener and hairdresser, at this address.

Middle Farm and Barn adjoining

(Grade II listed as "10a: Abbotsbury Smithy")

The building described here as "Middle Farm", with the red-tiled roof, is now the village smithy, originally opened just after the Appreciation was published, as part of the battle plan that brought the Dansel gallery and the pottery that has since become Abbotsbury Pictures.

The "Barn adjoining" (now no. 10a) has been turned into a furniture-maker's workshop.

10 West Street

(Grade II listed in 1956)

The Appreciation saw this as a working farm, describing the boundaries as including a *"stone wall with gateway into farmyard"*, though it was at one time simply listed as *"Cottage West of West End"*.

Interestingly in the light of the smithy apparently opened here in the 1970's, this house appears in the 1871 and 1875 directories as home to Henry Cheney, blacksmith, while the 1889 directory gives Edwin Bligdon as the smith here, and the 1903 and 1939 directories both list John Roper as the smith at this address.

West Yard and S.E. Building in West Yard

Stone building in West Yard

The Appreciation suggests that the SE building *"possibly should be listed - group value"*, but comments that the ten new concrete garages *"have a disastrous effect on the scene and should if possible be removed and replaced with more sympathetic buildings."* If they were new at the time, the doors don't seem to have lasted long ~ certainly not as long as the garages, which are still here after thirty years, albeit with new doors.

The whole of this extensive range was once the builders' yard for the Estate work force.

Unlisted it may be, but the Appreciation comments that it *"possibly should also be listed"*, and it has been put to significant use since the earlier photograph was taken. At one time, the left hand half of the ground floor was the office for H&J Designs, another example of the Estate turning over its redundant farm buildings for local craft use.

The left-hand door now opens to the control room and office of Abbotsbury Software and West Dorset Internet, which has pioneered several IT schemes, not least the provision of wireless broadband internet connection for the village and much of West Dorset, well ahead of BT installing broadband capability to the local exchanges.

Upstairs is the office of the Abbotsbury Heritage Research Project, which was granted £25,000 in 2004 from the Local Heritage Initiative to research all aspects of the village's history and set out the findings in a website. An auxiliary grant enabled the Project to design the website in a format that made it accessible to the visually handicapped, and a grant from Awards for All has made the free publication of this book possible.

The right-hand half of the building houses the offices of Abbotsbury Tourism, which markets the development of the Swannery, the Sub-Tropical Gardens and the various attractions at the Tithe Barn. The ground floor meeting room provides a base for local Estate and tourism staff conferences.

One thing hasn't changed ~ the puddles in the yard ...

West building in West Yard

1973 **2005**

The larger building, which the Appreciation thought should possibly also be listed, remains, but the *"temporary wooden garage and a corrugated iron shed (which) could also be removed with advantage"* have indeed been removed.

9 West Street and adjoining barn

1973 **2005**

(Grade II listed in 1956, formerly as "West End")

No. 9 (the house in the middle of the photographs) has a *"moulded stone from Abbey over door (St Nicholas)"*, and a distinctive single course of limestone above the windows.

The 1939 directory lists James White, insurance agent, at this address ~ one of the family from New Barn farm who retired into the village, the other two living in the 20th century houses at 12 West Street and 13 Rodden Row.

The single-storey "barn" on the right is currently (2006) to let, but was used by a local stonemason for a several years before the Estate turned it into office accommodation, when it was then used as the office for Abbotsbury Music. It thus joined the collection of redundant farm buildings put to similar use, in line with the "battle plan" drawn up as part of the 1973 developments.

8 West Street

1973

2005

(Grade II listed in 1956, also formerly listed as "West End")

No 8, or "Upalong" was one of the few Abbotsbury houses with a rendered front at the time of the Appreciation. Part of the description there adds details of the *"barn adjoining with corrugated iron roof, creosoted boarded E wall ... vertical boarded front wall with large double doors."* This was all that was left in 1973 of the filling station that once stood next door to no. 8: the pumps were later moved to the Swan Inn, but the thatched shop area was still standing, albeit ruinous, when the family who now live in 8 West Street moved in there.

The picture below, from Dave Stevens' collection, shows Joseph Hughes' garage that has been replaced by 1 Hannahs Lane (p. 88). For many years, 8 West Street was the home of Fred Lexster the swanherd, who had married Violet Hughes, the daughter of the garage owner.

In 1951, the District Surveyor was asked to extend the pavement beyond Hannahs Lane.

(loaned by Dave Stevens)

7 West Street

1973

2005

(Grade II listed pre-1974)

This is one of the confusing bits of West Street ~ the cottage on the right, with the dark door is no. 7, now showing a white door. No. 6, which opened from the white door that is no longer there included the windows on either side, and is now entirely incorporated in no. 7. That white door just happened to be white in 1973 ~ according to Muriel Page, it had been red, then green: it all depended on what colour paint the Estate had in stock at the time.

In the 1940's, Muriel Page was Miss Muriel Dunford (right), daughter of the local postman, living in no. 6. She later married Joe Page, and it was as Mrs Page that she gave the couple who live in no. 7 today the plan opposite of how the ground floor of her house was laid out in those days.

(loaned by Muriel Page)

The conversion of the two cottages into one took place In the early 1980's. Further modernised by an Anglo-Canadian couple in the 1990's, no. 7 looked rather like a patchwork quilt for a time while four different mortar mixes were left to dry and weather, so that the Estate could decide which of the four made the best blend with the older masonry of the adjoining cottages. As to why they differed, the reason lay in the amount of red ironstone that was added to the mix.

For the rest of the story, see across the page for the details of no. 6.

6 West Street and building adjoining

(Both buildings were grade II listed pre-1973)

As noted, no. 6 (the white door on the right) is now part of no. 7 ~ the "building adjoining" on the left was an infill at the time of the Appreciation, but is now part of no. 5. Both doors shown in the 1973 picture are now walled up.

As already noted, Muriel Page (née Dunford) has provided the couple who now live in the house with a plan of how her home looked in the 1940's (below).

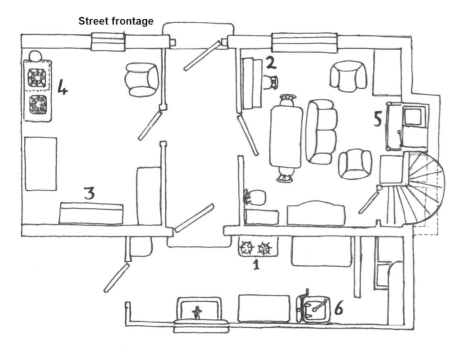

Apart from the conventional tables, chairs and cupboards, there was a piano (**2** on the plan) and an organ (**3**) ~ the Dunfords were a musical family.

Quite how far Abbotsbury cottages have moved on since the 1940s, may be seen from the "wooden stand for two primus stoves for heating water for bath and washing machine" (**1**), and the "paraffin fuelled two-burner cooker" (**4**), below, left ~ the "open fire and oven" (**5**), below, centre ~ and the "washing machine (**6**), below, right. Just note that the washing machine is hand-driven, complete with its own mangle ...

Upstairs were two bedrooms ~ and the toilet was, of course, outside.

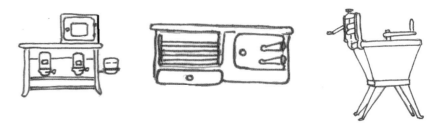

According to Muriel Page, the "building adjoining" was known as the "shop", but has now been incorporated into no. 5 next door. The photos below show no. 6 and the infill building dressed up for the 1953 Coronation.

(loaned by Muriel Page)

5 West Street

*(Now Grade II listed as 5 and 7 West Street,
formerly listed as "part of range of 5 cottages East of the Forge")*

Only a coat of paint, and what looks like a new thatch, separates these two photographs. The house was, however, modernised and extended at the rear at about the time the Appreciation was being written, though none of that work is visible from the street. This is only one of many Abbotsbury cottages which manage to have the best of both worlds ~ modern comfort in a very traditional shell.

Richard Vivian, harness maker, is listed here in the 1871 directory, and appears as a saddler in the 1889 one: the Joseph Vivian who appears in the 1903 directory as a saddler was presumably Richard Vivian's son. According to Muriel Page, the family were still living there in the 1950's.

4 West Street

(Grade II listed in 1956)

Apart from a new door, with its slated canopy, this cottage may seem to have changed as little as its neighbour ~ but all is not what it seems. Just glance across the page ~ ~

Methodist Church West Street

1973

2005

3 West Street

1973

2005

(Grade II listed in 1956)

The Methodist Church, one of two (there was a Primitive Methodist chapel off Red Lane) stood on the site of what is now the garage for the modern 4 West Street, itself an enlargement and extension of the original no. 4.

The photograph below is of a Remembrance Day gathering at the church in 1983, which one who was present believes to have been the last service held in the church. Some little time after that, the church was disposed of, as Methodist rules did not allow the building to be used for any other purpose, and no. 4 was extended into its grounds. Some of the initialled foundation stones from the Church were incorporated in the new building.

Peter and Hazel Evans of the Abbotsbury Heritage Research Project, have carried out a detailed study of all the Free Churches in Abbotsbury, and have posted their findings on the Project's website. *(www.abbotsbury-heritage.org.uk)*

The Appreciation describes this as *"Non-shop. Papers and veg. Racks outside door. Sign 'Fresh farm Eggs' swinging at E end of house."* It's still a non-shop, and a popular one at that, even if the newspaper business has moved down the road to Chapel Lane Stores.

Over one of the windows is an unusual plaque, dated 1747 and worded ~
"I x C
H x C
M x C"
Such plaques often indicate a marriage, but the appearance of three sets of initials is something of a mystery.

(loaned by Daphne Sheppard)

2 West Street

(Grade II listed in 1956 ~ formerly listed as "The Forge")

The Appreciation comments on the fact that the rubble ironstone walls are built to courses, and that the triple-light window at the side is made without window bars.   It is now numbered as 2a and 2b, but at the time of the Appreciation it was the farmhouse, owned by the Hutchings family, for West Farm, which covered the land to the north of Chapel Hill, with the field immediately behind the house producing huge quantities of vegetables.

West Farm: South West building

At the time of the Appreciation, no. 2 West Street was still West Farm, and these single-storey buildings were genuinely its outbuildings. They still form part of the curtilage for no. 2 West Street.

West Farm: South East building and outbuilding

These, however, are not what they seem: the "south east building" is actually a rear view of West Farm Barn, and the "outbuilding", described in all its awful glory opposite, was incorporated into West Farm Barn when it was turned into a house.

Barn at West Farm

1973 **2005**

*(Scheduled in the 1974 Village Plan as a building which
the Secretary of State had agreed to include in the statutory list,
with the note that it was "formerly included in the supplementary list")*

In 1973, this was indeed a barn, part of West Farm (now 2 and 2a West Street). Christopher and Daphne Jonzen moved here in September 1980, after 18 months of conversion work. The barn had been virtually derelict, and had a tractor shed (see the lower picture on p. 64) at the back, made out of a curious mixture of brick, breeze blocks and corrugated iron. Both buildings had been struck by lightning and the crack caused by one of the strikes is still visible. The thatch had largely gone, and the interior of the barn was a great open space, with the sky above visible through the gaps in the elderly thatch.

The plans drawn up by the Estate called for the tractor shed to be demolished and replaced with a new wing for the house. They also called for proper foundations, which involved digging holes a metre wide and deep under the walls before back-filling them with reinforced concrete, then digging out the spaces between the holes, inserting steel bars across the floor space and completing the work with a reinforced concrete floor. The thatch had next to be replaced. As a repair, rather than a change to the building, this was subject to VAT, but when what was left of the old thatch was removed, the rough wooden roof timbers were so dry and brittle that a completely new roof structure was installed. That meant a wall plate had to be put in place, lifting the entire roof by the 10cm thickness of the timber used for the plate ~ making the roof work an improvement ... and hence free from VAT.

The plans and the building regulations led to some complications ~ the new upper floor was only 3ft below the eaves, and the regulations called for a minimum ceiling height of 7ft, resulting in a very wide landing corridor; and as a result, some storage space that had not originally been envisaged.

Some of the proposals in the plans were rather unorthodox ~ the south wall of the new wing, facing Chapel Hill, was given only a tiny window, along with a hearth and chimney on an external wall. That was quickly changed for a large window with a superb view. Despite the fire planned for the new wing, there were no fireplaces in either the dining room or the kitchen, but one was proposed in the centre of the entrance hall, surrounded by a spiral staircase.

The conversion in 1980 was among the early changes that created new residential properties, and at that time, there were only half a dozen or so incomers, who formed the *"Abbotsbury Leaseholders Thatched Properties Association"* in order to secure a discount on a block insurance policy. The established villagers were more cautious then than they are now, but the couple were eased in by their friendship with the then Head Gardener at the Sub-Tropical Gardens, who wrote the annual village pantomime and created a part for Christopher as soon as the Jonzens were in residence. The pantomimes, performed in the then Reading Room by a very local cast, turned out to be an ideal introduction to village life, even if the incomers missed many of the in-jokes.

"West Barn" seemed to be the obvious name for the new house: it was only later that the occupants were told that a farmer called Wyndham had used the barn for many years ~ but it was then too late to change the name to "Wyndham's Barn".

1 West Street

(Grade II listed ~ formerly listed as "Rylands")

As already noted, when Abbotsbury houses were first numbered, Market Street, Rodden Row and Back Street were numbered in the conventional way, but for some reason, West Street was treated in a totally different way, so that no. 1 is almost opposite no. 50, something of a puzzle to relief postmen.

The house has a plaque over the door, dated 1782, and bearing the letters "WAM"

For years this house was occupied by Bill and Molly Cribb. The postcard below illustrates just how many ~ and how subtle ~ are the changes that have taken place in the village over the last near-century. No. 47 West Street (p. 44) was still intact, the school still had its bell tower, the Back Street stables were still thatched, and (this is why the photograph is here) 1 West Street had a pigsty in its back garden, and was linked to a little thatched barn on its right.

(loaned by Dave Stevens)

Chapel Farm thatched barn, and outbuildings

(Scheduled in the 1974 Village Plan as a building which the Secretary of State had agreed to include in the statutory list, with the note that it was "formerly included in the supplementary list")

Even if it were not obvious from the photograph, the barn's pretty sad condition in 1973 is clear from the description ~ *"... patched cement and sand ... 3 rough old wood (windows) ... yard in front overgrown grass"* ~ but the Appreciation sums it up as forming a *"splendid side to lane"*.

It became even more splendid when it was converted to (more precisely, rebuilt as) a fine house c. 1980. It changed hands when it was sold in May 2005.

Outbuildings north of Chapel Farm Barn

Furlongs Homestead

(Scheduled in the 1974 Village Plan as a building which the Secretary of State had agreed to include in the statutory list)

This outbuilding, once the milking parlour for Chapel Farm (the small shed in the 1973 photograph was the pasteurising room) was first turned into a pottery by Roger Ross Turner in the early 1980s. The business passed to Ray Lane, a potter from New Zealand, before it became Chapel Yard Pottery in 1990, where Richard Wilson still produces earthenware and stoneware, decorated in traditional slipware methods. After several years of running a gallery from Rodden Row, Richard has hopes of changing the site to provide for a house, along with a pottery and gallery.

The Conservation Plan describes this as *"a post-Enclosure homestead/farm re-located to the periphery of the village after re-apportionment of land, possibly positioned deliberately to obscure view of sunset from Abbey House."* (!) The authors suggest that, while it pre-dates the 1814 Enclosure survey, the barn comes from that era, implying that it was built in the early 1800's, with other parts of the farm added later in the 19th century. The homestead, they add, is almost completely free of 20th century additions.

1 and 2 Seaway Lane

(Unlisted in 1973, but "should be listed" according to the Appreciation, and now Grade II listed)

These two mid-19th century houses overlook the cricket field, which was given the 2005 Wisden award for the most beautiful cricket pitch in England.

The pitch and its predecessors have an interesting past. Lord Ilchester offered land to the village (not the current cricket pitch, but a field below the Chapel), in 1928 on a 10-year lease at a nominal rent for use as a recreation ground. When the lease expired in 1938, the Earl learned that the law prevented him from either giving the ground to the village, or offering it on a long enough lease for it to qualify for a National Playing Fields Association grant. He resolved the matter by selling the field to the village outright for £5.00 ~ and donating the money for the purchase, so that it cost the Parish Council nothing at all to acquire.

3 Seaway Lane

(Unlisted in 1973, but "should be listed" according to the Appreciation, and now Grade II listed like its neighbours)

The Appreciation describes this cottage as *"picturesque seen across ground from village"* ~ it's picturesque from pretty well any direction, and it even has the evocative name of "Smuggler's Cottage". It's handy enough to both the sea and the village to have served that purpose, and given that its origin is considered to be 18th century, it even dates from the right period.

House on site of station (Abbots Peace)

1973

2005

Old railway building

1973

2005

Opened in 1885 after lengthy controversy, the line (which connected to the main line at Upwey) was closed down in November 1952, long before the Beeching cuts. The first news of the closure came in 1948, by which time passenger traffic was low (even if the local school children depended on it), and the campaign to keep it open had few arguments in its favour. All the same, it was a sad day when the last train left Abbotsbury station, adorned with a wreath from the Parish Council.

The station was then demolished ~ the photograph below must be one of the last of the building to be taken ~ and the house which replaced it was built between 1962 and 1963. The Appreciation comments that the colour of the reconstructed stone is wrong, but excuses that on the basis that it is set well back from the road. In fact, it was a condition of the railway company that the house be made from the same Portesham stone as the original station, one low wall of which remains in the garden.

Ironically, the worst blizzards in years blocked the roads In January 1963, cutting Abbotsbury off from the outside world ~ *"Royal Navy helicopters from Portland had to drop vital supplies, a situation that never arose when the railway was running!"* (Brian Jackson: "The Abbotsbury Branch", Wild Swan, 1989)

The first owner of the new house was a Dorchester chemist called Tynegate, whose claim to fame is the invention of stage blood ~ stains from his world-patented mixture still adorn the walls of the garage ~ and the creation of especially bloody effects for early episodes of "Doctor Who".

This is one of the very few Abbotsbury Branch buildings still intact ~ it was the goods shed, just to the east of the village station. The large doors at each end were high enough to allow a passenger coach to enter, but the main purpose of the shed was to unload goods from wagons brought there (or allowed to roll there, as the line was on a falling gradient) via a siding, while the main traffic could go back and forward uninterrupted.

A second siding was available in Abbotsbury for goods that might take time to load up, and proved especially useful during World War II ~ *"wagonloads of ammunition were stored here well clear of Weymouth Harbour"* ~ not so clear, though, of Abbotsbury village itself.

(loaned by Dave Stevens)

69

House on south side of Weymouth Road
(Linton Cottage)

1 and 2 Grove Lane

*(Scheduled in the 1974 Village Plan as a building which
the Secretary of State had agreed to include in the statutory list)*

Named from Linton hill, visible in the background, and built c. 1925, this was once a police house, and has changed hands only infrequently since.   Now, greatly enlarged since 1973, it is a guest house.   The Appreciation describes it as *"ugly but screened by trees, though visible on way out of village"*. The photo on the right shows that, ugly or not, it is now so screened by trees that it is no longer visible ~ indeed, it is quite invisible ~ from the original viewpoint, even though it has more than doubled in size since 1973.

The Appreciation had a thing about the garage door, mentioning it three times and commenting that it marred the building ~ *"soldier brick arch and pine doors quite out of character"*.   Somebody was even then putting the matter to rights: the pine doors were painted almost immediately after the Appreciation photograph was taken, and the arch was later curved to match the windows.   The door below it is also painted white like the rest of the cottage woodwork.

The cottages are now combined, with the former no. 2 used for holiday lettings, and its original door converted into a window.

Abbotsbury Mill

1973

2005

(Grade II listed in 1956)

Barn opposite Abbotsbury Mill

1973

2005

The Mill probably dates from the 1600's.   The millers' wills exist from 1663, when Thomas Ham left enough money to care for his under-age son, provide for his son-in-law and other relations, as well as the parish church and the poor of the village.   Forty years later the miller Thomas Cole left money to those same families, but also shrewdly bequeathed to Richard Legg *"Fourteen pounds which I lent to him and yet remains in his hands."*

By 1749, the mill was in trouble: the millers lost everything they owned, right down to a basket and a pair of boots, to settle arrears of rent.   Ten years later, the Estate's bailiff blacklisted the people forbidden to grind corn here, forcing them to pay another miller to take on the job.

Successive millers in the 19th century left to run farms.   Jonathan Adams became miller in 1875, taking over from the Wallbridge family, but turned to farming in 1880. Three more millers followed until the Mill closed down in 1921. *"The old people can remember the mill when it was in use after the First World War: at harvest time the children used to be taken along in wagons to farms six or seven miles east or west of the village, and go leaving in the fields. Then they would take the corn down to the mill to be threshed, and feed it to the fowls at home. They remember the noise, the thumpety-thump of the mill machinery and the clackety-clack of the wheel".* (Jeremy Harte)

It was restored in 1971 by Margaret Berry, who also restored the Dairy House. The mill wheel dominates two floors of the conversion, described in the Dorset Echo at the time.   By 1984 it was taken over by Winifred Giles, a painter, and then passed to Guy East, a film producer whose credits include *Driving Miss Daisy* and *Sliding Doors,* and changed hands once more in 1997.

(Many thanks to Jeremy Harte for these notes.)

The sorry-looking barn has more of a history than one might guess, as it appears on maps as far back as the 18th century in connection with the Mill on the opposite site of Grove Lane.   It was converted into a holiday cottage in 2002, has been attractively landscaped since, and its location greatly brightened by the felling of the trees behind it.

3 Grove Lane

(Scheduled in the 1974 Village Plan as a building which the Secretary of State had agreed to include in the statutory list)

This may look like a 19th century 3-storey farmhouse, but Richard Simonds and Roger Ross Turner have uncovered a more complex history ~ they learned that the house had originally been single-storey (two rooms), that the first floor was not added until the 1700's and the top floor in the 1800's, with the single storey extension on the side and rear of the house. The barn had been the village bakery, but was closed in 1670, when it moved up to the village.

By the mid-1990's it was semi-derelict ~ there was plumbing only on the ground floor kitchen and the bathroom that the Army had installed during the war. Electricity extended to part of the first floor and no further. Plumbing, central heating and wiring were installed in 1997, along with damp-proofing, a new roof and top floor ceilings. The original roof beams were hand-carved oak in excellent condition, as were some of the windows and their frames.

In 1998, the barn was converted into a self-contained studio, and was found to contain the remains of three oven entrances. One of the barn walls, which defied drilling, turned out to be over four feet thick, and the floor level was below that of the house, presumably to make for easier loading of heavy sacks of flour. All attempts to remove a stout metal spike failed, until the later removal of a Victorian fireplace uncovered the other end of the "spike" as a bar across the depth of the much earlier fireplace, used for hanging pots.

The family are in the habit of calling out on coming home, to find out if any other member of the family is in. The unfamiliar voice which occasionally replies is the ghost *"of a woman in her 40s, dressed in a full length skirt, white shawl and tied back hair. .... We have all got quite used to her voice now. We have not seen her clearly although she has been seen by some standing by or going in or out of the back door."*

4 and 5 Grove Lane

(Scheduled in the 1974 Village Plan as a building which the Secretary of State had agreed to include in the statutory list)

This is one part of the village where the trees have grown up so much since 1973 (many elms have died in the interval) that it is next to impossible to photograph these two houses from the same viewpoint. Both houses have been extended since the Appreciation ~ the single-storey outbuilding on the north end has become a two-storey extension to no. 4, which may (along with some modern windows, and a 1997 loft conversion) explain why the building is not listed. The *"ruined wall at south side with corrugated iron shed"* became the new entrance (and a significant extension) to no. 5 in 1974 shortly after the Appreciation was published.

6 and 7 Grove Lane

*(Scheduled in the 1974 Village Plan as a building which
the Secretary of State had agreed to include in the statutory list)*

Built c. 1850, these were gamekeepers' cottages from the years before World War I until about 1980, were restored in 1997 and remain occupied by Estate staff and their families.

Old Kennels by Swannery car park

(Grade II listed)

The mid-19th century kennels were turned into a tearoom for the Swannery in 1995-96, and the kitchen was extended in 2004, to include the gabled area nearest the camera in the right-hand photograph.

Abbey House

Grade II listed in 1956 (as "Abbey farmhouse with shed and walling to east")

According to the Conservation Plan, this is a 17th or 18th century long house, suggested by its style and position vis-a-vis the "Malt House", and has been modified over the years, without amalgamation of earlier buildings (presumably contrary to the belief that it was once the Abbot's lodgings). In the same way, the boundary walls mark post-dissolution boundaries, and, as in Abbey House itself, the monastic stones visible are insertions rather than original features.

Abbey House was very much a farm in the 19th century, surrounded by allotments and greenhouses, but it boasted a croquet lawn and tennis court, and by the first half of the 20th century it was home to the three Misses Hawkins, daughters of the village doctor, and was later owned by Roger Ross Turner (son of the West Street potter), who researched and refurbished the house, which is now run as a guest house by Jonathan and Maureen Cooke. The gardens have been considerably changed since the Appreciation photograph, opening them up to lawns for guests and tearoom customers.

Abbey Workshop (Abbots Walk)

(Listed in 1956 as "Estate Workshop" ~ now Grade II* listed as "Abbott's (sic) Walk")

The building is described in the listing register as 14th and 17th century with 19th century arches. The Conservation Plan agrees that the North, South and East walls may be monastic remains, on to which have been added a 16th or 17th century South wall (the one in the photographs) and a two-storey garderobe in the NE corner.

It was used as a workshop by Estate staff until some time in the 1950's or 60's. The cart doors (now converted to windows) were inserted in the 19th century, and the roof was possibly rebuilt in 1973, when the one-time workshop was in the process of being converted into a private house ~ the 1973 photograph on the left clearly shows the work in progress, while the 2005 one on the right shows the result, complete with the roof work done in 2003-04.

The Conservation Plan suggests that this may have been lodgings or a service building for the monastery ~ it has been identified as the Abbot's Lodgings in published work since 1887, and there are burial sites close by. It was surveyed in 1938, but the survey missed the fact that the building tapers from east to west.

The building is called "Abbots Ward" in the Conservation Plan, and this is the name on the sign by the 1973 photograph of the Archway, but it is now known as "Abbots Walk". It remains a private house.

Archway across road to Abbey House and Workshop

*(Listed in 1956 as "Gateway 30 yards north of Abbey dairy",
now Grade II listed as "25 mtrs SSE of outer gatehouse")*

The listings register describes the Archway as having 14th century material re-used, and "re-used" is the significant term. The Appreciation describes it as a *"seventeenth century segmental arch. Probably gateway to house destroyed during Civil War"* and none of the other commentators see any reason to disagree. What is certain, too, is that it is *not* an archway from the Abbey precincts, though bits of it might have started from there.

The arch may have been linked to walls running north-south or east-west, but there is no obvious sign of how a gate might have been fixed. The archway resembles the inner porch arches of the tithe barn, but also the 17th century doors in the parish church. The Inventory places it as 17th century, and the Conservation Plan suggests that the arch is *"a deliberately antiquated structure of 17th century or later date ~ possibly a triumphal arch associated with the Strangways house ~ largely made of salvaged material."*

Abbey Dairy House

(Grade II listed in 1956, now listed Grade I)

"Dairy House" or "Gate House" ? It depends on your point of view. What you see from Church Street is the back of the house, not the front. It was originally a gate house ~ but to where ? "The Abbey precinct" seems the obvious answer, but English Heritage and the occupants' architect share the theory that it was the gatehouse to the original tithe barn. Mediaeval Abbeys were hugely rich, their storehouses functioned like banks and were protected by walls and nearby gatehouses. The room above the gateway here may have been the "chequer" where tithes were counted, similar to the room above the entrance to today's Tithe Barn which replaced an earlier barn.

Margaret Berry restored the building in the 1970's at the time the photograph on the left was taken, and turned it into two houses: hence the two "front doors" in Church Street, one of which is now inaccessible. It then passed to a solicitor, who removed the dividing walls, but never used the part nearest the village. He also held a paddock across the road from the Dairy House and part of the Manor House garden. A land exchange was agreed, by which the Manor House gained more ground and took on the care of the paddock.

The present occupants turned it into a family home in 1984, opening up the unused attic floor, building a detached games room, and entirely rebuilding the would-be garage as a traditional cottage once they realised it had no foundations.

The building had not been a dairy for years (the Council complained in 1948 about the state of the pavement here due to lorries collecting milk churns), and stood semi-derelict after years of being two separate cottages, so the 1970's conversion (which took two years and went well over budget) had problems ~ Mrs Berry was obliged to preserve the superb internal archway that had once been the gateway, and resolved matters with a spiral staircase and a mezzanine floor. That work has now gone, and the arch stands proud once more, though the restoration disturbed a swarm of bees which stopped work for two days.

continued overleaf

The family who live here believe that their house has three distinct parts. Looking at it from Church Street, the left and highest block is the original 14th century gatehouse with its two arches and gatekeeper's lodging. The outside steps leading to the first floor lodgings door (now a large arched window) have left indentations discernible on the outside wall. The southern buttressed wall shows signs of where the original wall enclosing the barn would have joined it. The northern internal wall of this section is also buttressed and even older, possibly as early as the 11th century, and is thought to have been the outside wall of an earlier barn, the far end of which was uncovered when the Manor House moved its drive and gate to its present position in the 1980's.

The right hand part of the house, nearer the village, is late 17th century, while the west wing, which for years blocked the large arch, is thought to date from the 16th or 17th century.

The Conservation Plan may differ on matters of detail, but the authors agree that the house has a medieval core and *"displays an immense quantity of archaeological and architectural detail"*, though the authors go on to suggest that it is just possible that the piers of the so-called "Outer Gatehouse" may have originally been part of the northern end of this building.

On a domestic note, the occupants comment that when they first moved in, the grounds of the Manor House with its tennis court, combined with their own unplanted garden with a 1970's swimming pool, marred the view from the Chapel, making Broad Meadow look as if it bordered a country club. Since then, trees and shrubs planted in both gardens, and the lake in the Manor House have concealed both eyesores, though adding considerably to the mosquito population.

The photograph below shows the northern frontage of the house before the 1970's restoration.

(loaned by Iris Trevett)

Farm building opposite Abbey Dairy

The Conservation Plan goes into more detail than the Appreciation, describing the building as a purpose-built piggery dating from the late 18th century, with a swineherd's office at the downslope end. (One wonders why Georgian swineherds needed offices, with neither VAT nor the CAP to trouble them.) There would originally have been open pens at the front of the building, with the low doors in the middle of the wall allowing access for the pigs and piglets into the open air.

Granary south of Abbey House

(Grade II listed as "granary 40m south of The Abbey Farm House")

The one thing this 18th century building is unlikely to be, according to the Conservation Plan, is a granary. It is too close to the pond for grain storage, and is built of rubble, which is not the usual form of construction in this part of Dorset. It is possibly (thanks to its detailed window frames) what the Conservation Plan calls *"a decorative addition to Abbey Farm, part of a Romanticisation of the landscape in the early 19th century"*. It is a shame that the upper windows have been blocked and the walls rendered, as it has the potential to be more attractive than it is at the moment.

Old Dovecote

(Grade II listed in 1956 as "Pigeon House", now listed Grade II*)

According to the Appreciation, its date of construction is *"uncertain. Probably Mediaeval origin much altered seventeenth and eighteenth century."* The Appreciation is right to use that word "uncertain" ~ the Dovecote does not appear on the 1814 survey, yet there is a building called "Dove House" at this location on the 1758 map, and the cross on the top of the little picture on the map hints at a link with the long-gone Abbey. The listings register plays it cautiously by describing it as 15th century with 18th century alteration.

According to the Conservation Plan, the fact that it does not feature on the 1598 and 1650 survey of tenant holdings could mean that it was held in-house by the Estate ~ the authors agree with the Appreciation that it may be mediaeval in origin, but renovated in the 17th and 18th centuries. Only the dormers and the rooftop lanterns are more modern. The building is in poor condition, thanks largely to what the doves have left in it over the centuries.

It has also had a varied history: in 1989 it might have formed a part of the "Kingdom of the Horse" centre when it was scheduled to move from its Lodmoor site in Weymouth, but English Heritage opposed the plan. At the moment, it forms a potential grandstand for the goat races at the Children's Farm based at the Tithe Barn.

Abbey Barn

(Grade I listed since 1956)

A tale of two halves. The **western** half, on the right is basically *"a 15th century tithe barn, much altered and refaced"* (the Conservation Plan) ~ the roof, however, dates from c.1700, when the tops of the walls might have been changed to allow the stone roof to be thatched. Before the alterations, possibly between 1760 and 1780, the parapet may have made the barn look even more like St Catherine's Chapel than it does from some angles today. JMW Turner picked one such angle when he painted the barn in 1795. This half of the barn housed a Rural Bygones Museum from 1991 until the contents were sold in 1996: after that, it provided a novel home for a Chinese Emperor's Terracotta Warriors until 2004, when the theme became the smuggling history of the coast, interpreted as an audio-visual display and a soft play area. At the time of writing, the barn is undergoing a major re-thatching exercise, using two seasons' harvest of local reed (12,000 bundles), significant timber repairs with oak from Melbury, and stonework repairs using limestone from a local quarry.

The **eastern** half has been roofless for at least 200 years, and has been repaired many times since. The wall dividing the two halves is 15th century in origin, and the barn may have been divided before the Dissolution.

The back of the barn has two puzzling features ~ a "cart door" in the south wall which opens to a hillside far too steep for any normal cart; and a slightly mysterious pit, not apparently part of a water mill, though the Conservation Plan wonders if the steps leading down into it may suggest that it was a pit used for treating wheat straw or withies. What adds to the mystery is that 19th century prints show a sizeable spread of water around this side of the Barn.

Cart shed and barn north of Abbey barn

1973

2005

(Unlisted according to the Appreciation, but recommended for Grade II listing)

A cutting-edge building in its day ~ the Conservation Plan describes it as *"an architecturally accomplished example of an 18th century 'Industrial Farm' building"*, perhaps a rebuilding of an earlier version, but in any case a *"forward-looking investment in the farm during the early modern period."*

The Appreciation comments that it *"partially obstructs the view of the Abbey barn from the village"*, but the trees to the north do that far more effectively today than they did in 1973. The building is now used as the ticket office and shop for the Children's Farm.

Range of farm buildings east of cart shed

1973

2005

(Unlisted in the Appreciation, but part recommended for Grade II listing)

The Appreciation was mainly interested in the range shown in these two photographs, and thought that at least part of it should be demolished, commenting that it obstructed the view of the Tithe Barn from the Abbey side and the church.

The Conservation Plan describes the whole collection of buildings, not all visible from this viewpoint ~ a mixture of style and dates from the late 18th to the early 20th centuries, with an element of uncertainty about it all.

This investment in the farm coincided, the Conservation Plan suggests, with the Strangways family link by marriage to the wealthier Fox dynasty in 1735 ~ Elizabeth Fox-Strangways (née Strangways-Horner), first Countess of Ilchester, inherited the estate in 1758, built Abbotsbury Castle and moved there in 1780, re-establishing the family links with Abbotsbury. It was at this time that Abbey Farm was developed and (so the Conservation Plan believes) later divided in two.

The 1973 photograph shows the pond in the process of being drained, as it was once again drained in 2004, though the Conservation Plan noted that at that time it was heavily silted up. The authors add that it is *"certainly artificial, but is not obviously related to any of the mills, so it may have been a fishpond."* That would tally with its location inside the Abbey precincts and the Benedictine dietary rules.

Remains of St Peter's Abbey : Pynion end

(Listed Grade II* in 1956)

Yet another mystery ~ the arch appears in 18th century views of the Abbey, but is missing from the 1814 survey, only 50 years later.

It was restored in 1846, heavily repaired in the 1920's, and was once more surrounded by scaffolding in 2005: but how old is it ? It is listed as 14th century, which puts it in line with the tower of the parish church, and might tally with a time of Abbey development, but there are several masonry schemes in the building, some of which don't tally with other buildings of similar age in the Abbey precinct. A 12th century stone, for example, is inserted in the back of the ground floor fireplace. The Conservation Plan comments that *"it may be part of the post-Dissolution house slighted during the Civil War ... or a folly.'* The Appreciation combines the two possibilities ~ *"Probably formed east wall of narrow building (perhaps a refectory), gable end with fireplace on west side and buttresses on east. Apparently incorporated in Tudor manor house built after dissolution and destroyed during Civil War".*

And "pinion" ? Nothing to do with cog-wheels ~ "pignon" is the French for "gable", but why it's not therefore called simply "Gable End" just adds to the mystery.

Remains of St Peter's Abbey: Outer Gatehouse

(Listed Grade II*)

Was this ever a gatehouse ? Despite the existence of 18th century views of a much more complete building than the fragments that remain, the Conservation Plan believes that it may be a 19th (or even 20th) century invention. The listing register says that it is a 14th/15th century fragment, with 12th century stonework inserted into the North wall extending to the West.

What is not shown in the Appreciation view from the north, but is clearer in the view included in the Conservation Study gazetteer, is that that the arch bases fronting the road are merely the ends of two walls running back from the road towards the cemetery on one side and the Manor House on the other: and it is the latter which prompts the speculation about its age.

According to the Conservation Plan, *"it corresponds with features recorded on the 1814 survey ... but the fabric appears largely rebuilt"*, including bits and pieces of 12th century decorated stonework inserted in the outer wall on the Manor House side in a way which *"suggests a date in the first half of the 20th century"*. Given that the Manor House was extensively restored in the late 19th century, and again at times between 1943 and 1982, could the whole gatehouse have been brought to its present shape as recently as that ?

One other thought ~ a casual glance at a large-scale map of the Abbey precinct, with a guess at where the west door of the Abbey Church might have stood, puts this gatehouse so nearly in front of that door that anyone entering the precinct from the village would almost have to double back in order to enter the church. But that's no more than a guess.

Remains of St Peter's Abbey: Abbey Malthouse

1973

2005

(Grade II listed in 1956 as "shed and walling to east", now Grade I listed "with attached walling")

Neither a shed nor a malthouse ~ it is in fact a water mill, as evidenced by the circular scoring marks in its inner wall from the mill-wheels. The confusing name may have been attached to this building from the 1650 survey, which includes a "Great Malting House" without identifying its location. On the other hand, it might have served several purposes at different periods in its history.

In 1662, Sir John Strangways (restored to his estates after the Civil War) granted a lease for a site "called or known by the name of the Abbey Mill", and it was still in action as a Mill in 1740, and appears on the Donne map of 1758, though it is not mentioned in Hutchings (1774). By 1801 the mill stream had been blocked, and by 1899 the building had been divided into two parts. Roger Ross Turner did some detailed research on the building while he lived at nearby Abbey House.

The 1867 edition of Hutchings has an illustration of buildings to the south of what is left, and the walls facing the car park (below) need to be considered as part of the Mill. The whole building presents some of the greatest challenges to conservation in the Abbey precinct alongside, perhaps, a great opportunity to open out and explain its original purpose.

St Catherine's Chapel

1973

2005

(Grade 1 listed in 1956)

A late 14th century building, perhaps put up in expiation for the blood-letting of the Wars of the Roses ~ built entirely of stone, including the roof, the only wood in it is in the doors. It was repaired in 1742, and again in the 19th century, and for a third time just before the Appreciation was published.

Why St Catherine? Apart from being the patron saint of spinners, philosophers, wheelwrights, and spinsters, she seems to have an affinity with hill tops: at least four Dorset hills boast a St Catherine connection. In reality, so far as reality counts with stories of saints, she was a 4th century Alexandrian girl (perhaps something of a bluestocking?) who successfully confounded the philosophers of her day and fobbed off the advances of the Roman Emperor, only to be martyred by being lashed to a wheel. Even then, she won the day when the wheel shattered, but it was a hollow victory and her body, so runs the legend, was transported by angels to the monastery on Mount Sinai which took her name.

It is the "spinster" connection that endears St Catherine and her Chapel to Abbotsbury ~ it is said (and it is firmly believed) that a visit to the Chapel, accompanied by the following prayer, is a sure-fire way of ending one's spinsterhood ~ ~

> Sweet St Catherine send me a husband.
> A good one I pray.
> But arn-a-one better than narn-a-one.
> Oh St Catherine, lend me thine aid,
> And grant that I never may die an old maid.

The Chapel has long featured in village celebrations ~ according to the *Sherborne Mercury*, it was once *"made to represent an English 74, with masts and rigging, and dressed with colours"* to celebrate the 21st birthday of one of the Earls of Ilchester.

continued

The unique setting and style of the Chapel has more than once attracted artists in many media. Tharp used St Catherine's for a sequence in a ballet made for TV and shown on "Arena", and in 2000, the Chapel played host to 48 banners (right) made by local businesses and community groups in the village as a Millennium celebration.

It is a regular stop-off point for groups from the Othona community near Burton Bradstock, who end their walks with a song here. The acoustics are excellent, and that might explain why some Dutch tourists once waited until the choir inside had finished, only to find the Chapel empty when they entered. As the wife remarked afterwards, "I have never seen my husband run so fast."

Though the Estate own the Chapel, English Heritage and the Dept of Culture, Media and Sport are its guardians and their permission was needed for the banners display. For all that, comparatively recent guidebooks invited visitors to the Chapel to contact the keyholder for access, offering a variety of possible addresses. It is now open daily during daylight hours.

There are occasional services here, attracting locals, visitors and "well-behaved" dogs: the last one each year is always on St Catherine's Day in November.

Margo Williams in *"Ghostly Gifts"* tells how she was able to free the spirit of an 18th century sailor, who had jumped ship with some stolen gold coins, and had dropped one by the Chapel. Ms Williams found the missing coin and released the sailor's ghost from its imprisonment in the Chapel. It is undoubtedly a spiritual place, witnessed by the recent growth of small offerings of flowers and prayer notes left in the little recess in the south wall.

Parish Church of St Nicholas

1973

2005

(Listed, according to the Appreciation as "Grade A" ~ Grade I listed in 1956)
(The listing includes a Grade I listed length of 15th century wall,
and the Grade II listed churchyard cross)

"If there is an architectural monument to the devotion of English parishioners around the Reformation, this is it." (the authors of the Conservation Plan)

It is not, however, the first Abbotsbury church: whatever was built here before the arrival of the Abbey in the 11th century lies beneath the site of the Abbey's high altar. This was originally a small church built by the monks for the village in the 14th century. Then the tower was added, and a century later the nave was lengthened. Just before the Dissolution in 1539, the nave was widened and arcaded aisles inserted into the enlarged building, making the interior quite lopsided in relation to the outside.

In the 17th century, a small door leading to the Strangways' house was cut in the south wall, and in the 18th century the gilded reredos was placed behind the altar. Two 19th century restorations bring the process up to date, with only minor cosmetic alterations in the 20th century.

The Conservation Plan makes the interesting point that the indifferent workmanship of the various additions over the centuries suggests that local parishioners would have been doing the work, thus fortunately allowing the church to escape the clutches of professional Victorian restorers.

Once the Millennium banners had come down from the Chapel, the designs were turned into half-cross-stitch patterns, and the men and women of the village stitched nearly 60 kneelers between May and December 2000, to give the church a permanent memorial of the Millennium. Five years on, a similar group of people ~ nearly 50 of them ~ are stitching a dramatic cover for the grand piano which is on permanent loan in the church.

Developments since 1973

There has been more change in Abbotsbury since the Appreciation than meets the eye, even if you discount the enormous changes wrought inside the cottages that have been renovated or modernised internally.

The Appreciation identified seventeen possible locations for development, seven of them by converting existing buildings, two by reinstating properties that had once existed, and eight through (more or less) infilling gaps. Of the seventeen opportunities, only seven have been taken up ~ three "prime infill" conversions (West Barn, Chapel Barn, and Whitehill Cottages) ~ three "secondary infill" sites (The Keep in Back Street, the houses between 42 and 43 West Street, and Bishops Close) ~ and one variation on a secondary infill proposal (Galway Cottages) which has been placed on a different alignment and in a different position from the original.

Perhaps it is just as well that the others went no further ~ if West Yard Barn had been turned into houses, Abbotsbury Tourism would have had to find another office base, and would the occupants of the house proposed for the top of Dansel's yard have welcomed the summertime stream of visitors around their front garden ?   The small cottage proposed for the back of the village green would surely have been in the proverbial "shady nook" even at the height of summer unless it replaced the trees around the green ~ and would anyone now seriously consider a *"new house ... on the low ground below Church Street to the west"* ?   In between the Manor House and the Dairy House, and right opposite the Arch ?   The omission from the proposals that seems most puzzling, however, is that the gaps between 24 and 26 Rodden Row and between 46 and 48 West Street have not been filled up.   One assumes that traffic hazards might have something to do with it.

In the event, eleven sites in the village have actually been developed over the last thirty years or so, in addition to individual houses on infill land ~ between them, the developments account for something like 50 new houses in a village which in 1973 only ran to around 130 properties.   Yet visitors still comment on the unchanging, timeless nature of Abbotsbury.

Included in the post-1973 developments have to be the new buildings to accommodate the needs of a growing tourist industry: included because at least three of the redundant farm buildings surveyed in the Appreciation have been turned over to tourist use, and others have been converted to commercial use.

Recent housing developments have concentrated on "affordable housing" and homes for local people, something that is not always easily squared with using traditional materials and building in the local vernacular style.   Further development will become progressively more difficult as feasible sites are becoming harder to find, with the development boundary being drawn more tightly around the existing edge of the village.

Note

Rather than try to list the new developments chronologically, I have followed the general plan of the Appreciation, and worked westwards through the village.

The map inside the back cover shows the location of the changes and the new developments.

Abbotsbury Glebe

© Simmons Aerofilms

The development answers to a variety of names, but the site was apparently always known as "Parson's Close" before the houses arrived.

Following a proposal from the Salisbury Diocese in 1988, a scheme was developed for an estate of 26 properties ~ 8 houses and flats for rent via the Raglan Housing Association, 8 for fixed equity shared ownership houses funded by Raglan, 8 houses for private sale by CG Fry (the developers of the estate) and 2 houses for rent remaining in the gift of the parish. This obviously involved a complex agreement between these parties, together with the Chesil Bank Parish Council and the West Dorset District Council. The foundation stone was laid in February 1992, and the estate was opened by the Prince of Wales in 1993.

It is said by one of the residents here that the work here gave Prince Charles the idea for the Poundbury development ~ he met Philip Fry, the son of the developer, who had served in the Navy, and was impressed with the way the houses had been built in traditional style and with the quality of the building work. As a result, CG Fry & Son won the contract for the first stage of Poundbury.

The photograph below was taken by Roger Pitman while the building was in progress in 1992.

(loaned by Roger Pitman)

St Catherine's Terrace

© Simmons Aerofilms

This group of six houses on glebe land was built at the same time (1992) as the Glebe development, and given the name "St Catherine's Terrace" by one of the first people to buy a house in the terrace.

Because the terrace is considered to be part of Rodden Row, residents in these six houses fairly regularly receive deliveries addressed to nos. 1 to 6 Rodden Row itself, a confusion which neither the Post Office nor the courier firms seem to be able to resolve.

The photograph below shows Prince Charles at the opening of St Catherine's Terrace in 1993.

(loaned by Rosemary Rees)

Bishops Close

1940s

2005

© Simmons Aerofilms

Galway Cottages

2004

2005

Bishops Close, intended as bungalows for the elderly, was under construction in 1973, just after the Appreciation was published. Peter Fell comments, on the view looking north from Rosemary Lane, that *"the proposed old people's bungalows to be built above this corner will have to be of the highest architectural quality to succeed. The siting above the road will be difficult to handle, but a 'fragmented' group will allow the scale to be kept down to match nos. 3 and 5."*

At least one of the residents (now in her twentieth home, so she's in a position to judge) describes Magna Housing Association as a helpful and efficient landlord, recently replacing the original draughty wooden window frames with double-glazed units, and another newly-arrived resident still can't get over the extent of the storage space available in what seems from the outside to be a fairly conventional small bungalow.

Planned since 1999 amid some controversy, building began in 2004 on this terrace of three one-bedroom cottages, managed by Weymouth & Portland Housing Association for the Estate as affordable housing for local people. The site was one suggested by the Appreciation for infill, but at that time the Back Street terrace had yet to be built and the Appreciation was also suggesting a car park on what are now allotments in the lower part of Back Street ~ the idea was to build three separate houses facing south in what are today the back gardens of the Back Street terrace pictured overleaf.

The left-hand photograph shows the site just before the builders moved in, and the picture on the right shows the completed terrace. The photograph below (left) was taken by Roger Pitman during the construction of the cottages, and the computer-created picture below (right) is the architect's impression of the finished terrace, more or less identical to the actual building, though the reality seems to stand a little higher above the horizon than the intention.

(loaned by Roger Pitman)

© The Lawray Partnership

8 and 10 Back Street

Despite being numbered as two houses, there are in fact four maisonettes here, built in the mid-1980s in conjunction with Magna Housing Association.

12 to 22 Back Street

These six cottages, built by Hastoe Housing Association, were completed in 1992 under an agreement by which the landowner (in this case the Estate) gave the land free of charge, or for a small payment well below the market price. The houses would then be sold or rented out for lower than the usual rate, thanks to grants from the Housing Corporation.

The houses were intended to be sold on a shared equity basis with a covenant restricting them to local people, or were rented ~ in either case, they were to be made available to people carefully vetted to be sure that they were in need. Those who rented the houses were given security of tenure for their own lives and those of their families.

One of the younger residents of the terrace is Robin Snuggs, who survived a premature home birth during the NHS strike in 1989 (with the journey to hospital in an Army ambulance and a police escort) to go on to reach in 2005 the second place in the UK Pro Men's Kitesurfing division.

The Keep

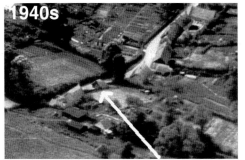 

© Simmons Aerofilms

This was one of the sites that the authors of the Appreciation singled out in 1973 as a "secondary site for infill building", adding that *"in our opinion careful thought would need to be given to design in these sites to ensure that the buildings do not detract from their surroundings"*.

Plans for the house were drawn up in 1980, and the architects were well aware of what could go wrong ~ *"A new cottage replica could be built at high level .... This would be an extremely difficult site to handle. The existing barns on the lane could be included with the site for garaging or storage."* The architects knew what they were up against because they were Messrs William Bertram and Fell, the very architects who had drawn up the Appreciation.

Conditions attached to the building were strict ~ everything facing the road had to match the surrounding buildings, which at that time meant only the traditional cottages of Back Street; the stone and slate had to be local, and the angle of the roof, even though it was slated, had to reflect the angle of a thatched roof, resulting in a fine array of exposed beamwork. The Scandinavian origins of the husband of the first couple to live in The Keep resulted in a very well-insulated property when it was handed over in 1982.

The barns in front of the house were once a butchery business and on the land behind the house are the remains ~ old stonework, and a drainage channel ~ of what might once have been the slaughterhouse for the business. The shop and the one-time stable are pictured on p. 22.

Copplestone

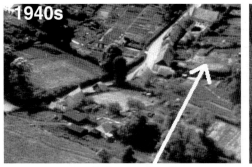 

© Simmons Aerofilms

Copplestone was built in conjunction with the houses (1 to 3 Whitehill Cottages) that replaced the nearby old barns and workshops fronting Back Street, pictured on p. 24. Built, like the cottages, by Michael Still to a design by his architect Clive Hawkings, the house was built by Roy Copp, a local mason.

According to a feature in *Country Life* in 1992, *"despite the planners' reservations, Still realised, correctly, that this higher ground needed a large house to provide the necessary weight."*

Copplestone is not just a large house ~ it is one painstakingly made from entirely local materials, including a massive stone chiselled lintel which may have come from the Abbey. For the more functional stonework, Roy Copp and Michael Still made their own hydraulic stone cutter to produce regular 6" blocks from the stones taken from the Back Street barns described on p. 24 and also used a number of beams from the old barns, to preserve, in Michael Still's words *"as much of the antiquity as possible."*

Dairy House lodge

1984

2005

Built in 1984 on the site of a ruinous outbuilding which the occupants of the Dairy House intended to turn into a garage. Once they discovered that the old building had no foundations, the plans had to become more ambitious, and an almost entirely new dwelling arose on the original footprint.

1 Hannahs Lane

1930s

2005

(loaned by Dave Stevens)

At one time, Abbotsbury had its own filling station, Hughes' Garage, which closed down many years ago ~ the pumps were taken to the Swan Inn, and were still there when the Appreciation was compiled, attracting some adverse comment from its author.

The whole site was redeveloped in 1996 ~ the slate-roofed shop to the right of the pumps has become the blind wall on the right of the modern photograph, while the thatched building behind the pumps has been replaced by the double gate and high courtyard wall of the new house. Despite the numbering which puts it in Hannahs Lane, the entrance is in fact in West Street. The present occupant has been told that the thatched building on the lane was once a butcher's shop and that the lane was originally known as "Butcher's Lane".

Hannahs Lane terrace

Chestnut Cottage

At the time of the Appreciation, Hannahs Lane was an overgrown footpath leading down to Seaway Lane.   Once the long-departed filling station went, to be replaced by 1 Hannahs Lane, the logical consequence seemed to be a small terrace of cottages alongside the now wider roadway, and these houses went up in 1997.

The 2003 West Dorset District Local Plan places the development boundary close against the edge of the terrace, which implies that these three cottages are not going to be the start of any encroachment south towards Chapel Hill.

One question remains ~ who was Hannah ?

The Appreciation photographs seem to suggest that the lane leading to the cricket field was in those days a wider thoroughfare than Hannahs Lane, yet it has remained what it was thirty-odd years ago ~ a lightly-used route to a local amenity and no more.

Chestnut Cottage was built in 1998-99, just after the Hannahs Lane terrace, using a mixture of local Abbotsbury, Purbeck and Portland stone.

24a West Street (Rakers)

Built in 1987 as one of a pair with 24b, and completed in late May 1988. The land was previously used as a steep sloping allotment for no. 23, and many hundreds of tons of earth were removed to level the site. The house is faced with stone from a quarry near Beaminster, which is comparable in colour to the traditional Abbotsbury stone used in the village. The occupants greatly appreciate the uninterrupted views over their garden to farmland, Ferny Hollow and the Ridgeway to the north.

24b West Street

Also built in 1987, the house was bought when it was still only a pegged-out site on the strength of the view of the village on a fine March day, and has been occupied ever since by the same family.

Development at Sunnyside, West Street

© The Lawray Partnership

As a complete layman, I like the way the Estate's architects have solved the two problems of this site.   To the west, the houses stand much higher than the houses on the east; and while the immediate neighbours on the west are rather dominant urban Victorian Gothic houses, the neighbours on the east are much nearer the Abbotsbury scale.   Though they may not all be thatched, the over-riding impression of West Street is one of thatched cottages.

The solution is a cascading terrace of cottages, firstly linking the two heights by letting the roofline drop parallel to the ground level, then linking the styles by building in local stone under thatched roofs, and finally linking the frontages by having the new development make a change in orientation to align it with its neighbours on either side.

The houses are intended to go on sale on long leases.

West Lodge

West Lodge was one of the early (but not the first) developments to follow the Appreciation. An advertisement for its sale on a century-long lease refers to the recently-won planning permission (presumably in 1988) for the Abbotsbury Glebe development, and goes on to comment that the house *"adheres to Abbotsbury's architectural code .... The materials are of exceptionally high quality, because the estate kept a feudal eye on every stage of its construction, even insisting that the garage was built first so the builders could prove they understood the Abbotsbury way of doing things."*

That said, the development was not universally welcomed at the time ~ it was said that it was out of scale with Abbotsbury's cottage scene, and for technical reasons, it had to be located differently from the original plan; but it has almost blended in to the landscape, and only from some viewpoints does its size stand out.

Swannery Visitor Centre

(loaned by Dave Stevens)

Sub-Tropical Gardens Visitor Centre

The Swannery "shop" reflects the increasingly commercial approach to tourism in the village ~ visitors expect something professional, and the car park with its overflow, together with the shop, the tearoom converted (and enlarged) from the old kennels, and the children's play area, are the least the Estate could do to accommodate the massive flow of visitors every season. It's all a long way from the days when one parked in a lane and slipped the swanherd a tip for a conducted visit, which is what might very well be happening in the left-hand photograph, taken in 1914 when the Dutch steamer *Dorothea* grounded on Chesil Beach ~ she is just visible in the background towards the top left-hand corner of the photo, one of many in Dave Stevens' collection.

The Gardens have developed apace in the last decade. At the time of the Appreciation and even in the 1980's when the left-hand photo was taken, visitor amenities were pretty minimal ~ a small shop for plants and a wooden cabin for teas and coffees. But to raise visitor numbers to the present 70,000 visitors a year called for something more ambitious, and the purpose-built visitor centre with a greatly enlarged plant centre was the result.

Sub-Tropical Gardens Café

1980s

2005

The little tea kiosk in the left-hand photo lasted until the late 1990's, together with a raucous pair of peacocks who appealed to and intimidated visitors in equal measure, but the end of the century saw the development of the "Colonial Tea House" in 1998 (and the departure of the peacocks).

The gardens are in the middle of a development programme lasting at least a decade, following an expansion in the early 1980's which followed the original intention of the first Lady Ilchester two centuries ago. In 2003, the Gardens served as the setting for a tropical island for the BBC TV production of Trollope's *"He Knew He Was Right"* with Geoffrey Palmer and Geraldine James, as well as hosting a German film production of a Rosamund Pilcher novel: in the following year, the staff were given the task of gathering fallen leaves for use in the fourth Harry Potter film.

In that same year, 2004, the largest project since the Gardens were first created was begun ~ the creation of a magnolia walk with 100 trees grown off-site on behalf of the Estate by the RHS gardening team at Wisley in Surrey at a cost of £50,000. When open, the walk will, for the first time, open up a view of the Fleet, the sea, and the recently designated World Heritage coastline from the Gardens and, for a short season, will provide a spectacular show of blossom.

INDEX of LOCATIONS

This book will be placed on the Heritage Project website

(www.abbotsbury-heritage.org.uk)

later this year, to allow for updates as more information comes in.

TWO LAST WORDS

Any opinions expressed here are entirely mine ~ unless they are obviously a quotation from some other source, which I shall have acknowledged.   If I have left anything out, I apologise.

The whole book will be updated with new information from time to time, in an internet version which will eventually appear on the Abbotsbury Heritage Research Project website.

www.abbotsbury-heritage.org.uk